MEASURES OF THE CAPITAL STOCK IN THE IRISH MANUFACTURING SECTOR, 1945–1973

Copies of this paper may be obtained from The Economic and Social Research Institute (Limited Company No. 18269). Registered Office: 4 Burlington Road, Dublin 4.

IR £5.50

(Special rate for students IR £2.75)

R.N. Vaughan is a Lecturer in the Department of
Political Economy in University College London.
He was formerly a Research Officer in The Economic and Social Research Institute. The paper has
been accepted for publication by the Institute,
which is not responsible for either the content or
the views expressed therein.

MEASURES OF THE CAPITAL STOCK IN THE IRISH MANUFACTURING SECTOR, 1945–1973

R.N. VAUGHAN

ISBN 0 7070 0037 8

Acknowledgements

I am indebted to E. Henry, J. McGregor, and B.J. Whelan for aid in the construction of the computer program on which basis the capital stock estimates were generated. I am further indebted to E. Henry for the use of the worksheets relating to investment purchases and sales.

The preparation of the tables and graphs was considerably aided by K. Thompsett. The paper was copy edited for publication by B. Payne and M. McElhone to whom I express grateful thanks. The comments of E. Henry and G. Hughes on an earlier draft of this paper and those of two anonymous referees are also greatly appreciated. The usual disclaimer applies.

CONTENTS

LIST OF TABLES

LIST OF FIGURES

Figure

GRAPHS

Graph

General Summary

The aim of the present study is the construction of a series of measures of the capital stock for the Irish manufacturing sector over the period 1945-73, along with associated values for depreciation and capital consumption. Capital stock data may itself have intrinsic merit as an indicator of the economic progress of an industry or manufacturing sector over a particular period; perhaps more importantly such data may be used in a variety of economic and business enquiries into the performance of various aspects of the economy. From the viewpoint of national economic policy, in so far as it is in the interest of government to direct or encourage, by fiscal or other means, investment in particular industries, then it is desirable that information concerning the productivity of existing investments in those industries be considered. Thus we may note the importance of the use of capital as a measure of input into the process of production. Using capital stock in this connection, the economist may be investigating reasons for the economic growth (or decline) of either an entire economy, or a sector of that economy. A second utilisation of capital estimates concerns enquiry into the profitability and rate of return on capital employed in particular industries; in this connection we may be concerned with the efficient allocation of limited financial resources. A third major interest is with the projection of aggregate demand. In so far as investment may constitute an appreciable proportion of domestic demand within an economy, then evidently, knowledge of the structure of the existing capital stock, and the likely distribution of capital retirement (and so replacement investment), may be an important factor in predicting total investment, and hence total aggregate demand.

In any economic enquiry, the concept and hence derivation of a capital stock series should be tailored to meet the requirement of the theory that is developed. However, for the most part, this is impractical, and theorists either have to define "capital" in relation to the available data, and develop the appropriate theory; or else stick to their original definition with an appropriate warning when they come to test their hypotheses that the measured variable does not correspond exactly to that required by the theory. However, two broad definitions of capital appear to have covered most requirements, the measures of *net* and *gross* capital stock. Both net and gross capital may refer to the same collection of physical items; however, different "price" or "weighting" systems are used in their estimation. The

1

definition of *net capital stock* is that measure of the capital stock which reflects the current market worth of capital employed; hence (for perfect markets) we have the implied valuation of capital at prices which vary directly with discounted future net output of each item of capital. The definition of *gross capital stock* is that measure of capital which reflects the current productive potential of capital employed. Thus it is appropriate that the "price" used to calculate this measure should be assumed to vary in relation to the efficiency of capital goods as measured by current output, rather than in relation to the prospective outputs of those goods. When we come to operationalise the net and gross concepts, the assumptions relating to changes in efficiency are embodied in the *depreciation* profile which attaches to the different components of the capital stock.

The *Perpetual Inventory (PI) Method* is a procedure for constructing net and gross estimates of the capital stock essentially via the summation of a series of investment expenditures with appropriate subtractions for depreciation and sales of capital. Such a method is particularly appropriate for the case of Ireland, since alternative estimates, e.g., via a census or sample survey of firms over a period of time, simply do not exist. Data requirements for the construction of capital stock estimates are a series of investment expenditures for different types of asset (inclusive of second-hand purchases and sales); appropriate price deflators, and knowledge of average lifetimes of different types of capital equipment. In the case of Ireland, the basic data series on investment expenditures and the initial capital stock are derived from the Census of Industrial Production (CIP) for the period 1945-73. Estimation of the average lifetimes are based on depreciation figures published in the CIP for the years 1945-50 in association with the depreciation rates and implied lifetimes as established by the Revenue Commissioners for the purposes of company taxation. Sales and purchases of investment goods in current value terms are placed on a constant price basis (1958=100), with indices derived from the appropriate CSO wholesale price series, apart from the price index of land which uses recent work to update the index used by Henry (1971). In addition, it was necessary to transform the initial capital stock from its published CIP book value to reflect a measure of gross capital stock at replacement cost new; the associated net capital stock value was also estimated. The expenditure series were also adjusted to include estimates of the investment of new firms. Second-hand purchases and sales of assets were entered at their appropriate gross or net valuation with an appropriately reduced average lifetime relative to new purchases. For estimates of gross stock, investments are retained in the series throughout their working life at original cost (in constant price terms) and then retired; whilst for the net stock, assets are linearly depreciated to zero over their lifetime.

On the basis of the above information, estimates of the capital stock for 50 designated industries of the Irish manufacturing sector are presented, together with additional information on Gross Fixed Capital Formation by type of capital good for 10 industrial sectors. An indication of the changing structural balance of the Irish manufacturing sector is provided by the percentage distribution of the gross and net stocks over the 10 sectors. As between 1953 and 1973, there has been a relative shift away from Sectors I-VI, namely, Food, Drink and Tobacco, Textiles, Clothing and Footwear, Wood, Printing and Paper, toward Sectors VII-X, Chemicals, Minerals, Metals and Miscellaneous (incl. oil refining). A marked increase in the growth rate of all sectors over the period 1963-73 as compared to 1953-63 is evident; the growth rate for all manufacturing increased from 5.0 per cent to 8.1 per cent (in terms of gross capital stock) on a yearly basis as between the two periods, with a spread of rates as between 3.0 per cent for Clothing and Footwear and 8.4 per cent for Miscellaneous Manufactures during the period 1953-63, and a corresponding low-high spread as between 5.2 per cent for Printing and Paper and 13.3 per cent for Minerals during the period 1963-73. As implied by the structural change noted above, growth rates were highest in sectors VII-X over both decades.

The study, in the light of the above newly constructed capital series, then contrasts the results with previous Irish studies, namely, the works of Nevin (1963), Kennedy (1971) and Henry (1971). We note the similarity in trends of the series of Henry and those of the present study, although the measures were constructed under quite different assumptions regarding depreciation, lifetime of assets, and valuation of the initial capital stock. All the studies agree that a structural shift to a higher trend in the growth rate of the capital stock (however defined) occurred in the period 1959-61, although the trends of the Henry series and those of the present paper appear as rather more pronounced than in the Nevin-Kennedy studies. The divergence in trends may be partly explained by alternative assumptions concerning treatment of the initial capital stock, and the subsequent effect of its depreciation on the future measures of net capital accumulation.

Finally, the study considers the drawbacks of the PI method, in particular the rigidity of the investment behaviour implied by the fixity of the distribution of investment expenditures in any given year as between "expansion" and "replacement" investment. However, it is argued that the "Capital Stock" variable generated by a PI model may be viewed as a special case of a general economic model in which the *cumulation* of a particular variable over time influences current economic actions. Thus the interpretation of the PI "capital" stock as a "constructed" variable in the statistical sense, may allow us to avoid a number of criticisms usually attached to a capital measure; i.e., we explicitly view it as an imperfect variable reflecting a given lag and weighting structure over past investment values and price indices.

The capital stock estimates presented in this paper, it is hoped, will provide a useful data source for further studies of the Irish economy. The categorisation by manufacturing industry and sector is fully compatible with the grouping of other statistical indicators for industry as published in the Census of Industrial Production. The use of capital information in conjunction with such data as gross and net output, and employment, therefore should aid future enquiries concerning productivity and industrial growth in Ireland. The importance of adequate information in this area has now been officially recognised in most advanced industrialised countries with the extension of the National Income Accounts to embrace additional data on capital stocks and flows. The present study, and the computer model upon which it is based, may provide an adequate framework upon which further development work on the Irish capital stock may proceed, and which may be updated as additional information on capital purchases and expenditures by industry becomes available.

Chapter 1

Aims and Purpose of the Study

1.1 Introduction

In this paper we propose to estimate, via the Perpetual Inventory (PI) method, gross and net stock measures of the capital stock in the Irish Manufacturing sector, along with associated values of depreciation and capital consumption. The measure of capital is restricted to fixed capital in plant and machinery, vehicles, buildings, and land. Working capital, including inventories and work in progress is not considered; neither are intangibles such as "goodwill". Coverage is restricted to those private firms or public enterprises which take part in the Annual Census of Industrial Production; the time period covered being 1945-73, although information for certain industries is only available from 1950 onwards. The data is presented by industry and by sector according to the "ISIC" classification in use by the Central Statistics Office since 1953.

The organisation of the paper is as follows. In this chapter we propose to consider the various alternative definitions of the capital stock, and the different bases on which the capital stock series may be generated. In Chapter 2 we outline the standard PI model of the capital stock, and the necessary modifications required for its utilisation in respect to the Irish data. In Chapter 3 the basic statistical series required for the derivation of the Irish capital stock estimates are discussed, along with approximations to the lifetime of assets, and the necessary price indices. In Chapter 4 we present estimates of the gross and net capital stock and associated measures of depreciation and capital consumption, for fifty industries, and ten major industrial groupings. In Chapter 5, previous estimates of the Irish capital stock are considered and contrasted, where such is possible, with the new estimates. Finally, in Chapter 6, the deficiencies of the PI method are considered, and possible future avenues for research are noted.

1.2 The Measurement of Capital

In many applications of economic theory, the researcher starts with well-defined concepts of the variables that enter the problem under consideration and then may attempt a search of the statistical literature for measures of these desired variables. However, in many cases, the theorist cannot approach the problem of data collection, *ab initio*, but has to be content with the data that have already been collected either by statistical agencies or other private investigators. Thus is raised the problem of a disjunction between the theoretical concept that it is desired to measure, and the actual concept that is being measured by the available statistical series. If the researcher is unable to construct a series which measures exactly the concept that interests that person, then one should either construct a theory in which the concepts used are those that are empirically measurable, or there should be provided a bridge between the desired and measurable concepts in terms of mathematical relationships. In practice, this may rarely be done and consequently "hybrid" theories are constructed and tested in which theoretical concepts are equated to empirical measures of the same "name" irrespective of whether there is any close relationship between the underlying variables. Such a procedure may lead to difficulties in the interpretation of results, inconsistencies in the theory and to predictive falsehoods. Naturally, this mismatching of "ideals" and "measures" occurs in many areas of empirical work in economics (or indeed in scientific measurement in general); however, particularly acute cases may occur in the area of capital measurement.

The avowed aim of the present exercise is the construction of a series of capital measures for Irish industry; whilst the exercise has intrinsic merit in its own right, e.g., in considering the progress of an industry, major interest may be concerned with the utilisation of capital stock series in a number of economic enquiries. It is therefore important that the different concepts of capital to be used in such studies should be distinguished and the appropriateness of the measures constructed in this study for such applications also be considered. We should, therefore, stress that the choice of a measure of capital may depend not only on the accuracy of the underlying data but on the relevance of the data for a given analytical use; and capital stock data may indeed be used in a variety of economic and business enquiries into the performance of various aspects of the economy.

(i)   As a first example we may note the use of capital as a measure of productive input into the process of production. Using capital stock in this connection, the economist may be investigating reasons for the economic growth (or decline) of either an entire economy, or a sector of that economy. Capital stock estimates in this connection, for example, may be used in a regression of a measure of output on capital and other productive factors.

(ii)   A second utilisation of capital estimates is an investigation into the profitability and rate of return on capital employed in particular industries or firms. In this case we may be concerned with the efficient utilisation of financial resources.

(iii) A third major concern is with the projection of aggregate demand.

In so far as investment may constitute an appreciable proportion of domestic demand in an economy; investment demand being composed both of additions to the capital stock, and replacement investment — then evidently, knowledge of the structure of the existing capital stock, and the likely distribution of retirements may be an important factor in predicting total investment, and hence total aggregate demand.

These three uses, which we may categorise into the production, financial and investment demand aspects, may be viewed as constituting the major utilisation of capital stock series. Given such diverse applications of the data, are different measures of the capital stock required? Ideally, as we have noted in any economic enquiry, the concept and derivation of a capital series should be tailored to meet the requirement of the theory that is developed. However, for the most part, this is impractical: and theorists either have to define capital in relation to the available data, and develop the appropriate theory: or else stick to their original definition with an appropriate warning when they come to test their hypothesis that the measured variable does not correspond exactly to that required by the theory. However, two broad definitions of capital appear to cover most requirements, the net and gross measures of the capital stock.

1.3   Net and Gross Measures of the Capital Stock

In the literature one finds two well established definitions of the capital stock, viz., the gross and net stock measures. Both may refer to the same collection of physical objects, but as time changes, may show marked differences in their development. Thus suppose the economist seeks an answer to the problem regarding the changes in output engendered by a variation in the stock of capital utilised in the production of that output. Provided physical units of measurement are used in the exercise, then the relationship is governed by technology; however, when various types of good are aggregated via a "weighting" procedure, then certain anomalous results may appear. Thus, for example, even during a period of constant absolute prices, the relationship between net capital stock and the value of output may not be unique in the sense that a declining net capital stock may engender no changes in the value of output, at least over the measurement period. This would arise from the fact that although the physical efficiency of the machines may be unimpaired over the period of observation leading to no decline in output, the market value of the machines will certainly fall assuming that they have a fixed lifetime, and that prospective buyers of the machine are influenced by the future profits that such a machine could earn. Thus, if we are interested, say, in measuring variation of yearly output consequent on changes in the capital employed; utilisation of competitive market prices for the valuation of capital, leading to an estimate of the "net capital", may appear rather inappropriate, since variations in this measure of capital need not reflect changes in the physical capacity of the capital employed. Thus alternative "price systems" or "weighting systems" may be employed in estimating the capital stock, the choice of which depends on the use to which the measure of capital is put.

In the case where we wish to measure the "gross capital stock", i.e., in relation to production studies, it is appropriate that the price of the capital good should be assumed to vary in relation to the efficiency of that good as measured by current output, rather than in relation to the *prospective* output of that good.

In the case where a measure of capital is desired to reflect the current market worth of capital employed, then valuation at prices which vary directly with discounted future output, is required, i.e., the "net capital stock" concept.

When we consider the relationship between the Gross and Net Stock measures for the economy, then naturally, the relationship will vary according to the temporal structure of the capital stock. The Net Stock cannot, of course, exceed the Gross Stock, provided consistent measures of valuation are used. As should be apparent from the above remarks, the gross stock gives a better approximation to the current productive capacity of an economy's capital, whilst the net stock, at a given date, reflects the potential output of this stock. In this paper, we propose to derive estimates of the gross and net stock concepts, and associated measures of depreciation and capital consumption. The formal relationship between the net and gross stock measures will be outlined in the next chapter; before doing so let us note the major approaches to the measurement of capital, and a brief survey of the current literature on the subject.

1.4 Approaches to the Measurement of Capital

The two essential inputs into the measurement of a capital stock are (a) a catalogue, if possible, of the different types of capital good in quantum terms and (b) the construction of a price or weighting system by which this heterogeneous collection may be aggregated. The literature pays more attention to the collection of data on (a); data on (b), except for the case of market prices is somewhat scarce, and is viewed principally as an artifact of the theorist.

Regarding (a), the following are among the methods that have been suggested:

(i)   A census of Physical Assets

  (ii)   A census of Insured Values
  (iii) A census of Book Values
  (iv) The Perpetual Inventory Method.

Methods (i) — (iii) require a survey of firms regarding the volume or value of assets employed in the firm. Insured values differ from book values in that the latter are usually depreciated original cost, whilst insured values of assets may be expected to approximate rather more closely the current valuation of the asset. Historic (Book) Values represent the valuation of capital at depreciated original cost, distinguished from Current Valuation, which includes adjustment for price changes. Method (iv) differs from (i) — (iii) in that it attempts to construct from details of purchases and sales of assets, the capital stock, dependent on a particular price system.

Apart from (i); methods (ii), (iii) and (iv) already assume a given price system within their calculation; thus unless we have knowledge of the time structure of the capital stock, it is impossible to transform from one valuation to another. This problem is particularly acute for (ii) and (iii), however, in (iv) we are usually given purchases and sales of assets in terms of current prices. The usual procedure is then to deflate these values to a constant price series, and then to treat this series as the quantum series to which subsequent price adjustments are made.

The four methods should not be taken as necessarily independent methods of estimation: e.g., (i) in conjunction with (ii) or (iii) may give information on the price adjustments made. Nevin's (1963) estimates of the Irish Capital Stock are essentially an amalgam of methods (ii), (iii) and (iv). All four methods necessarily involve a survey of firms. The most commonly used method in practice is (iv) the PI method.

With respect to the manufacture of a price or weighting system, i.e., input (b) noted above, we require prices to vary directly with the efficiency of the capital good (gross stock) or with prospective output (net stock). The usual assumptions here are with respect to a given life for the unit of stock, with an appropriate "depreciation function". The major requirements are, therefore, knowledge of the life of equipment together with the shape and parametrisation of the depreciation function.

The method of "estimation" of the capital stock we propose to follow in this work is that of perpetual inventory (PI), and such a model will be outlined in the following two chapters. However, before considering the technicalities of the problem, we may put the estimation procedure into perspective against the wider economy. In Figure 1.1 we have indicated for a simple economy, a conceptual scheme whereby the PI method relates both to the estimation of the capital stock and the theory of investment behaviour.

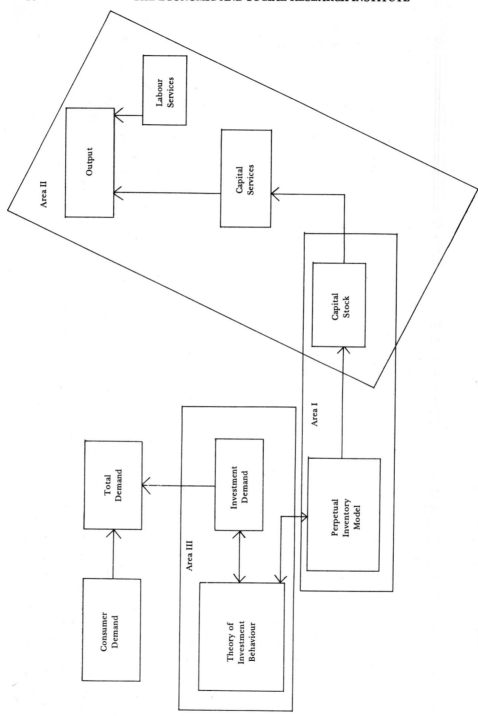

Fig. 1.1 *Conceptual Relationships between the Perpetual Inventory Method, Estimation of the Capital Stock, and the Theory of Investment Behaviour.*

This position will become clearer in the next chapter; however, we may here emphasise the point that one cannot choose independently any of the bases linked directly by arrows in Figure 1.1; i.e., a theory of investment behaviour implies a given PI model (or alternatively that a choice of a given PI model implies a given theory of investment behaviour). A given PI method implies a given capital stock (although not conversely). If one is not aware of the interlinkages, then inconsistent theory and estimates may be generated. Such inconsistency may arise because in many instances, the generators and users of capital stock estimates are not the same individuals. We have indicated in Figure 1.1 three broad areas of research which are apparent in the literature:

I. Development Work on Capital Stock

The work in this area is primarily of a "national accounts" nature; in many countries, construction of capital stock indices is by government statistical officers or agencies, based on data of sales and purchases of investment goods. Such estimates are usually straight applications of the PI method (see Ward (1976) for recent discussion). The major drawback of such investigations is the neglect of the economic theory of replacement and expansion investment.

II. Production Studies

A second area of research uses capital stock data as an input into the study of output, productivity growth, etc. The usual errors in such studies may arise from misunderstandings regarding the definition of the capital stock, e.g., the use of net stock estimates where gross stock might be more appropriate, or vice versa.

III. The study of Investment Behaviour

Investment Behaviour, including assumptions regarding depreciation, may serve to determine the capital stock via the PI method; likewise the capital stock, via its influences on replacement investment, will serve to determine investment demand, and thus its own evolution. In this area, mismatching is most likely to occur, since in many cases the capital stock is simply taken as a datum rather than as a derived series in such studies. The most common mistake is to assume that replacement investment is, say, proportional to the capital stock, whereas the capital stock itself has been generated on the basis of entirely different depreciation assumptions.

Jorgensen (1971) cites a number of such instances, e.g., with regard to Evans (1967), Jorgensen notes that the implicit depreciation function used for the derivation of the capital stock series is not consistent with the mortality distribution for investment goods assumed by Evans, "so his treatment of replacement investment is internally inconsistent" (Jorgensen, op. cit., p. 1123). Such inconsistencies have also arisen in Ireland, e.g., Geary, Walsh and Copeland (1975) assume proportional depreciation of the capital stock, whilst using a measure of capital constructed by Henry (1971) which is based on different depreciation assumptions; Glass (1971) in his use of Jefferson's (1968) capital stock estimates for Northern Ireland also has a similar problem of mismatching.

Chapter 2

A Model of the Evolution of the Capital Stock

2.1 Introduction

In the previous chapter we have considered the various definitions of capital, and their appropriateness for specific analytical tasks. In this chapter we propose to concern ourselves with the mechanics of the derivation of such series, and the informational requirements that are necessary for their construction.

The construction of capital stock estimates via the perpetual inventory (PI) method is essentially by the summation of a series of investment expenditures, with appropriate subtractions for depreciation and sales of capital. Complexities may arise with respect to the treatment of price and quality changes, insufficient length of an investment series relative to the service life of an asset, and the correct treatment of purchase and sale of second-hand assets. The intimate relationship between the perpetual inventory method and the theory of investment behaviour arises from the fact that the PI method relies on estimates of gross investment, i.e., Gross Fixed Capital Formation (GFCF). Thus, in order to cumulate our investment expenditures over time and arrive at an estimate of the capital stock we have to have knowledge of the split of GFCF between replacement and expansion investment, i.e., a theory of investment. We shall note below how alternative investment theories lead to alternative estimates of the capital stock.

2.2 A Simple Method

We begin with a simple model of the capital stock in which problems of aggregation, price changes, and valuation of second-hand goods are neglected. We take as the basic equation governing the evolution of the capital stock: (2.1), i.e.,

$$K(t) = K(t - 1) + IE(t) \tag{2.1}$$

$$I(t) = IE(t) + IR(t) \tag{2.2}$$

$K(t)$ refers to the capital stock at the end of the year t. $IE(t)$ as expansion investment, or net capital formation occurring during the year t. Thus capital at the end of year t equals capital at the end of year $(t-1)$ plus the net additions to the capital stock that have occurred during the year. Total investment $(I(t))$, or GFCF, equals expansion investment $(IE(t))$, plus replacement investment $(IR(t))$ as is specified in equation (2.2); all investment occurring during the period $[t-1, t]$.

An equation such as (2.1) may therefore be solved recursively, subject to an initial condition on the capital stock, to give

$$K(t) = K(0) + \sum_{j=1}^{t} (IE(j)) \qquad\qquad (2.3)$$

which on substituting for (2.2) gives

$$K(t) = K(0) + \sum_{j=1}^{t} (I(j) - IR(j)) \qquad\qquad (2.4)$$

where $K(0)$ is the initial value of the capital stock. Thus determination of the capital stock in any period requires knowledge of the initial capital stock, and expansion investment expenditures since that date. However, the information that is customarily available only refers to the $I(j)$, with possible independent estimation of the capital stock at infrequent intervals; thus we require a theory of the determination of $IE(j)$ (or $IR(j)$), with appropriate definition of the residual from (2.2). In PI calculations, it has usually been the rule to calculate $IR(j)$, $IE(j)$ being viewed as the residual, replacement investment being related to retirement of the existing stock.

In presenting the theory of replacement investment we may follow the analysis of Jorgensen (1971). Let the proportion of investment goods acquired in period t and replaced in period $(t+j)$, $j = 0, 1, 2 \ldots$, be given by $\delta(j, t)$. For a time homogeneous process, the replacement proportion depends on the period after purchase, not on the date of purchase itself; and so under this assumption $\delta(j, t) = \delta(j)$ all t; then the replacement over time may be described by the sequence: for $0 \leqslant \delta(j) \leqslant 1$.

$$\delta(0), \delta(1), \delta(2), \ldots,$$

where,

$$\sum_{j=0}^{\infty} \delta(j) = 1$$

Thus replacement investment in any given year is a weighted average of past gross investment, $I(j)$; i.e.,

$$IR(t) = \delta(D)\, I(t) \qquad (2.5)$$

where $\delta(D)$ is a power series in the lag operator D.
Hence from (2.1)

$$(1 - D)\, K(t) = I(t) - \delta(D)\, I(t)$$

i.e.,

$$K(t) = \frac{(1 - \delta(D))}{(1 - D)}\, I(t) \qquad (2.6)$$

i.e., the current value of the capital stock can simply be seen as a function of past levels of the gross investment series.

The construction of $K(t)$ via the above formula is thus somewhat "mechanical". Replacement of capital depends only upon the age of the equipment and does not vary from period to period, consequent on the availability of investible funds, strength of demand in the economy, etc. Dependent on the choice of the lag structure $\delta(D)$, different estimates of the capital stock may be developed.

2.3   The One-Horse Shay Estimates

Under the one-horse shay assumption, investment equipment has a fixed life, θ; capital retains its productive capacity throughout its life; and we have replacement investment at time t equalling total investment of θ years earlier. Thus in terms of the above model $\delta(j)$ is the series

$$\underbrace{0,\ 0,\ \ldots\ldots\ 0, 1,}_{\theta}\ 0\ldots\ldots$$

where unity constitutes the $j = \theta'$th term. Hence from (2.5),

$$IR(t) = I(t - \theta) \qquad (2.7)$$

and hence, from (2.6),

$$K(t) = \frac{1}{1 - D}\, I(t) \quad - \quad \frac{1}{1 - D}\, I(t - \theta)$$

$$= \sum_{j=0}^{\infty} I(t - j) \quad - \quad \sum_{j=0}^{\infty} I(t - j - \theta) \qquad (2.8)$$

$$= \sum_{j=0}^{\theta-1} I(t-j)$$

(2.8) continued

i.e., the capital stock in use is simply the sum of investments over the years of life of the asset.

The measure denoted by (2.8) is termed the gross capital stock; relative to this concept, we consider two additional notions; those of the *net capital stock*, and *capital consumption*. If an asset is properly maintained and retained its full value until it was ultimately scrapped, then capital consumption would be simply represented by the assets going out of use, and net investment would represent the difference between new assets installed and existing assets scrapped. This is the measure for "expansion investment" that we have:

i.e., Net Investment = IE(t) = change in the gross capital stock.

However, this measure of net investment takes no account of the ageing of existing assets prior to scrapping. It may be remembered that the essence of a productive asset is that it provides services over a long period. Thus there follows the accounting solution that the services of an asset, embodied in its initial purchase price, should be spaced equally over the life of that asset. Hence, relative to the gross stock measure:

$$K(t) = \sum_{j=0}^{\theta-1} I(t-j)$$

we have the net stock measure,

$$KN(t) = \sum_{j=0}^{\theta-1} \left(1 - \frac{j}{\theta}\right) I(t-j) \tag{2.9}$$

Analogous to the measure

$$IE(t) = K(t) - K(t-1)$$

i.e., net "gross capital" formation, we have the measure, relative to the net capital stock

$$IN(t) = KN(t) - KN(t-1) \tag{2.10}$$

as net "net capital" formation.

Analagous to the measure of assets discarded for the gross measure

$$IR(t) = I(t) - IE(t) \tag{2.2}$$

we have what may be termed "capital consumption", defined by

$$IC(t) = I(t) - IN(t) \tag{2.11}$$

This reflects, as compared with (2.2), not only the influence of the replacement of existing capital stock, as it falls out of use, but also the "consumption" of existing capital that has not yet been retired.

It should, of course, be stressed that the "one-horse shay" retirement pattern is an assumption which may be found to be mistaken should an empirical study of such patterns be undertaken in Ireland. We have followed British practice in this respect, assuming as does Redfern (1951) in his estimation of the British capital stock that "the productive services of an asset are likely to be more nearly constant over time than to decline exponentially."

Before applying such concepts to industries or firms, there are a number of complicating factors to be taken into account. We consider these as relating to:

(i)   comparability of purchases of investment goods at different points in time. Major reasons for differences in comparability being the rate of inflation or quality changes;

(ii) allowance for the sale as well as purchase of investment goods;

(iii) consideration of second-hand purchases;

(iv) the treatment of the initial capital stock, i.e., a problem which occurs when data on the investment series are of insufficient length to calculate the estimates, the period of observation being less than the average life of the good in question.

We shall consider each in turn, and the appropriate modifications to the above estimation procedure.

2.4 Comparability of Investment Goods Over Time

The aggregation of investment goods over time is somewhat analogous to that of aggregation of investment goods at a particular point in time. In both cases the price system may be used to advantage. In the case where the type of capital good being considered does not physically alter over time, then we may be concerned solely with correction for the price of the good. The price of a capital good may equal its cost of production, inclusive of the profit element; it may also equal the discounted value of the future profits to be engendered by that machine; the two being brought into equality via demand and supply; as demand and supply for identical machines shift from period to period, so ordinarily may the price of the machine.

Using market prices for the purchases of investment goods and simply summing such purchases over time (subtracting for depreciation (if net stock) and retirements (if gross stock)), a capital stock measure at what may be termed "historic cost" is generated. Such is the method that has been followed in commercial accounting practice. Such a measure would not, however, accurately reflect the efficiency of the stock as regards output potential — i.e., more weight is given to the costlier machines although their contribution to output is the same as the other machines.

An alternative to "historic cost" accounting is therefore "constant cost": in this case, the series on investment expenditures is first deflated to a base year. Capital stock is then measured on a particular year's prices; the resultant series may then afterwards be reflated to give "current cost" estimates.

The relationship between "historic cost" and "current cost" estimates of the capital stock, is not without interest, e.g., in transposing a balance sheet from an "historic" to a "current" cost basis for the purpose of company analysis. Let $I(t)$ denote investment at deflated prices, the price index relative to base year given by $P(t)$, then investment in terms of current prices is given by $P(t)I(t)$. Using the continuous time formulation we have for the capital stock at historic cost,

$$V_H(T) = \int_{t=0}^{t=T} P(t)I(t)F(t, T)\, dt \qquad (2.12)$$

where $F(t, T)$ denotes the proportion of capital stock purchased at time t retained at time T. Capital stock in current value terms is given by,

$$V_C(T) = P(T) \int_{t=0}^{t=T} I(t)F(t, T)\, dt \qquad (2.13)$$

The relationship between historic and current cost will depend on the course of price changes over the period, and on the time structure of investment purchases, and little can be said, in general, on this matter, except that in a period of continuing inflation, $V_C(T) > V_H(T)$. In the case where $P(t)$, $I(t)$,

F(t, T) are known analytic functions, then it may be possible to express the relationships in algebraic form. Thus, e.g., if inflation and growth proceed at constant rates h and g, and F(t, T) is of the exponential form, i.e.,

$$V_H(T) = \int_{t=0}^{t=T} P_o e^{ht} \, I_o e^{gt} \, e^{-\delta(T-t)} \, dt \qquad (2.14)$$

then we may show that,

$$\frac{V_H(T)}{V_C(T)} = \left[\frac{e^{(g+h+\delta)T} - 1}{e^{(g+h+\delta)T} - e^{hT}} \right] \cdot \left[\frac{g+\delta}{g+h+\delta} \right] \qquad (2.15)$$

2.5 Sale of Investment Goods, and Treatment of Second-hand Goods

The example we considered above has only been concerned with the purchase of new equipment: industries are therefore constrained to dispose of their equipment only through retirement. In actuality, however, firms may sell their plant and machinery, either for scrap, or to other manufacturers. In addition, firms may buy second-hand assets; thus in estimation of the capital stock it may be thought appropriate to consider such eventualities.

In fact, most studies of the capital stock for countries other than Ireland have not considered explicitly the treatment of second-hand assets. It is usual practice to deduct sales of equipment in a given year from purchases in that year, and thus the investment purchase series in Table 2.1 would represent "net purchases". Of course, in that case, net purchases may become negative, if sales of equipment exceed purchases in a given year; which may happen, e.g., in a declining industry. Similarly, purchases of second-hand goods are agglomerated with new purchases and treated on an equivalent basis. Ignoring the special properties of second-hand goods may, however, lead to errors. As noted by Hibbert, *et al.* (1975) commenting on existing British capital stock estimates: "The estimates of gross capital formation from which the perpetual inventory is compiled represent net expenditure (i.e., purchases less sales) on plant, machinery and vehicles, together with expenditure on new buildings and works. If a firm in industry A sells second-hand equipment to a firm in industry B, the net expenditure of industry A understates the value of new assets acquired by that industry and the net expenditure of industry B includes as though it were new the value of the second-hand assets acquired".

Thus errors both of valuation in respect to potential output of a machine and with respect to the age structure of the machines in service, may occur. We, therefore, propose to transform the data in an attempt to bring about comparability of second and first-hand purchases and sales.

We assume the following:

(a) The purchase or sale price of a second-hand asset reflects the true value of that asset; i.e., the value embodied in a second-hand purchase or sale reflects the "net capital value" of that item of plant or building.

(b) The age distribution of second-hand equipment is known. The simplest assumption is, e.g., that second-hand equipment is bought or sold halfway through the asset's life. For the purpose of discussion we shall follow this example; however, in the actual computation we assumed that 50 per cent of second-hand purchases and sales were bought or sold halfway through the lifetime of the asset; whilst each remaining 25 per cent were bought or sold a quarter and three-quarters way through the lifetime.

Under the above two assumptions we can transform the second-hand data into their gross and net stock equivalents. The treatment can be seen with the aid of Figure 2.1.

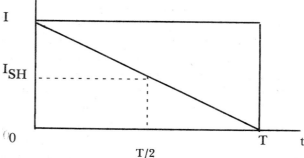

Fig. 2.1: *Gross and net stock valuation of investment over time with lifetime of length T*

Consider an investment of value I made in year zero, with length of life T. Then, according to the gross stock measure, I units are retained in production throughout its working life. Now consider the net stock concept, which approximates the sale or purchase price of the asset during its life. This is described by the linear depreciation curve from I at $t = 0$, to zero at $t = T$. Thus a purchase of this item of capital stock at age, e.g., $T/2$, should properly enter the Net Capital Stock at value I_{SH}, whilst for equivalence with assets purchased new, its entry into the gross stock should be at value I.

Such treatment may be contrasted with the "net purchase" treatment commonly used in capital stock studies. In this case the second-hand purchase is treated identically as a new purchase; i.e., it enters both net and gross stocks at the value I_{SH}, and the lifetime of the asset remains T. Second-hand purchases thus have two values, the monetary value, reflecting the net-stock value, and the equivalent gross-stock value, reflecting the output potential of the equipment at a given date. In constructing a table reflecting investment and the capital stock, therefore, two measures of Gross Fixed Capital Formation (GFCF) are necessary to reflect the "Gross" and "Net" Valuations, hence our two series GFCF(G) and GFCF(N).

Table 2.1: *Proposed Schema for the Generation of Gross and Net Capital Stock Measures*

Year	Gross capital formation GFCF (G) I(t)	Retirements IR(t)	Change in gross capital stock IE(t)	Gross capital stock K(t)	Gross capital formation GFCF (N) I(t)	Capital consumption IC(t)	Change in net capital stock IN(t)	Net capital stock KN(t)
	(1)	(2)	(3)	(4)	(5)	(6)	(7)	(8)
1	300	0	300	300	300	100	200	200
2	300	0	300	600	300	200	100	300
3	300	0	300	900	300	300	0	300
4	300	300	0	900	300	300	0	300
5	300	400	0	900	300	300	0	300
6	300	300	0	900	300	300	0	300
7	0	300	−300	600	0	200	−200	100
8	0	300	−300	300	0	100	−100	0
9	0	300	−300	0	0	0	0	0

Note: I(t) = IR(t) + IE(t);   I(t) = IC(t) + IN(t);
IE(t) = K(t) − K(t−1);   IN(t) = KN(t) − KN(t−1)

The above Table 2.1 indicates the relationship between the measure of GFCF, capital consumption and the capital stock.

In Column (1) we have the measure GFCF(G) which denotes GFCF relative to the gross capital stock. It denotes the sum of new investment plus the purchase of second-hand assets at equivalent new valuation.

In Column (2) we have the value of the gross stock which is discarded; this is the sum of gross stock retired from use at the end of its working life plus the gross equivalent value of the second-hand sales.

Column (3), the change in the gross stock, is thus the difference between Col. (1) and Col. (2) and Column (4) is simply the cumulation of Col. (3).

Similarly, we have a set of measures relative to the net capital stock concept. Column (5) gives the measure of GFCF(N), which denotes the sum of new investment expenditures, plus the purchase of second-hand assets at their net valuation.

Column (6) denotes capital consumption, the value of assets which are written-down in equal yearly portions over their lifetimes, plus sales of second-hand assets at their net values. The difference between Columns (5) and (6) is then net capital formation, the change in the Net Capital Stock (Column (7)), the cumulation of which, of course, constitutes the estimate of the Net Capital Stock (Column (8)).

In our example in Table 2.1, we have assumed an average lifetime of three years; the example is also simplified by the assumption that the value of second-hand goods purchased and sold is zero for the years concerned. Furthermore, in this example, the capital stock is generated from a zero base level. The corresponding representation for actual Irish data may be found in Table 4.1 below.

2.6. Treatment of the Initial Capital Stock

If, given the desired starting date of the capital stock series, the length of the time series of GFCF prior to the starting date exceeds that of the life-time of the assets concerned, then no additional information with respect to the initial value of the capital stock is required. However, this is rarely, if ever, the case and hence additional "start-up" information is required. In the case of Ireland, for the years 1945-50, the CIP besides publishing information regarding purchases and sales of assets also included data on the book value of assets of different industries. It is this information we shall use as the starting point of the capital stock series; however, before such data can be used for the purpose at hand, a number of transformations are necessary.

(a)   Transformation of Book Value Capital to Replacement Cost Capital

The data on plant and machinery, buildings, etc., contained in a company's balance sheet, and upon which the CIP estimates are based are not appropriate for many of the uses for which capital stock estimates may be desired. In the present case, we are attempting to measure the Gross Capital Stock at replacement cost new, and the net capital stock relative to this concept. Book values are not wholly comparable for two major reasons:

(i)   Book values generally represent the capital stock of a company measured at historic cost, i.e., the written down values of original purchase prices of assets remaining in the company's ownership are simply added. In a time of constant prices then there need be no difference between historic and current valuations, thus book values would represent the "net capital" valuation of the capital stock. In times of changing prices, then the book values represent an amalgam of various price levels, and the usefulness of the measure for productivity and efficiency analysis is consequently diminished.

(ii)   The second major difference concerns the depreciation practice of companies, in so far as the rate at which investments are written off, e.g., to maximise tax allowances, need not correspond to the diminution in the market value of the asset.

In the present study it is therefore necessary to bring the book value estimates as close as possible to our desired definition of gross and net stock. Of course, such a manipulation could only be done correctly with knowledge of a company's accounts, and reference to the purchases and sales of its assets. However, we shall attempt to derive appropriate magnitudes for these factors.

(b)   Transformation from Net Capital Stock to Gross Capital Stock

To transform from a net capital stock to a gross stock basis (under constant price conditions) we require information on both the depreciation factor used and the time structure of purchases of the assets. Under the assumption of linear depreciation over a lifetime $(T - L)$, and replacing actual investment in each period by the mean investment throughout the period $\bar{I}$, then the net stock figure is given by

$$NS = \int_{L}^{T} \left(\frac{t - L}{T - L}\right) \bar{I}\, dt \qquad (2.16)$$

$$= \tfrac{1}{2}\, \bar{I}\,(T - L)$$

and the gross stock is simply

$$GS = \int_{L}^{T} \bar{I}\, dt = \bar{I}\,(T - L) \qquad (2.17)$$

Hence from (2.16) and (2.17), GS = 2NS, i.e., to arrive at an estimate of the gross stock we simply double the net stock figure.

However, there appear two major reasons why such an approximation may not be wholly valid. In the above approximation we have replaced the stream of investment purchases $I(t)$, $L \leqslant t \leqslant T$, by the mean for the period

$$\frac{1}{T - L} \int_{L}^{T} I(t)\, dt = \bar{I}.$$ However, $I(t)$ may be subject to wide variation.

Thus in a time of continuing growth in $I(t)$, then certainly GS < 2NS, and conversely, in a time of declining investment expenditures, GS > 2NS. In our practical implementation of the model, we are dealing with the stream of investment expenditures up to 1945, upon which information is not available. It may be difficult to substantiate continuous growth in investment throughout this period, 1920-45; certainly, for new firms setting up in business, growth in investment in the late 'twenties and early 'thirties is likely, but such investment was not likely to be maintained in the late 'thirties and the war years.

A second reason for an approximation error concerns the date at which the major components of an industry were set up. In the above formula we have assumed that the lifetime of the industry is longer than that of the equipment therein employed; letting $T - X$ denote the lifetime of the industry, i.e., $T - X > T - L$. If this is not the case, then it can be shown that the relation between the gross stock and the net stock is given by,

$$GS = 2 \left[\frac{1}{2 - \frac{(T - X)}{(T - L)}} \right] \qquad NS \leqslant 2NS \qquad (2.18)$$

for $(T - X) \leqslant T - L$.

In the case of Ireland, relative to $T = 1945$, it is indeed possible that many industries lie within $T - X < T - L$, consequently we have another factor working towards $GS < 2NS$.

In the subsequent analysis, we propose, however, to take the bound of 2NS. The alternative would be to have factors differing across industries and across types of equipment. Further, we may have the compensating factor with respect to the time stream $I(t)$ that could be pulling GS upward towards 2NS.

(c) Transformation from an Historic Cost to Current Cost Basis

From (2.18) it may thus appear that we simply use the Balance Sheet figures as an estimate of the Net Stock, and double the figures for an estimate of the gross stock. However, these estimates are made on an historic cost basis, and we require a replacement cost basis. The difference arises, as already noted, from changes in the price level. We thus require knowledge of the price profile of investments prior to T. It would appear that mild deflation occurred in the period 1926-38, whilst there was a marked inflation between 1939-50. Splitting up our period into one of constancy of prices and then of inflation, and assuming that investment purchases (in real terms) are set at their average level throughout the period, then for the Net Capital Stock at Historic Cost we have the formula:

$$NSH = \int_{L}^{W} P_o \overline{I} \left[\frac{t - L}{T - L} \right] dt + \int_{W}^{T} P_o e^{g(t - W)} \overline{I} \left[\frac{t - L}{T - L} \right] dt \qquad (2.19)$$

Here we have taken the period up to W to be one of relative constancy of price, inflation at the rate g deemed to have occurred between W and T.

The formula for the Net Capital Stock at current prices (i.e., at time T), is given by;

$$NSC = P_o e^{g(T-W)} \int_L^T \overline{I} \begin{bmatrix} t-L \\ \overline{T-L} \end{bmatrix} dt \qquad (2.20)$$

and hence we may deduce the relationship between NSH and NSC as,

$$\frac{NSH}{NSC} = \frac{(W-L)^2}{(T-L)^2} e^{-g(T-W)} + \frac{2}{(T-L)^2 g} \left[[T-L-\frac{1}{g}] - e^{-g(T-W)}[W-L-\frac{1}{g}] \right] (2.21)$$

Thus the factor that must be applied to NSH can be seen to be dependent both on the rate of inflation and the lifetime of the good in question.

(d) Depreciation of the Initial Capital Stock

In addition to the calculation of the initial capital stock both in gross and net terms, we require the contribution of this stock to capital in subsequent years, letting NS(T) and GS(T) denote the values of net and gross stock at time T, then assuming no investment in subsequent years, we have

$$NS(T+J) = \int_{t=J}^{t=T-L} (1 - \frac{t}{T-L})\, \overline{I}\, dt \qquad (2.22)$$

and,
$$GS(T+J) = \int_{t=J}^{t=T-L} \overline{I}\, dt \qquad (2.23)$$

and, hence,

$$NS(T+J) = \frac{[(T-L)-J]^2}{(T-L)^2} NS(T) \quad 0 < J \leqslant T-L \qquad (2.24)$$

$$GS(T+J) = \frac{[(T-L)-J]}{T-L} GS(T) \quad 0 < J \leqslant T-L \qquad (2.25)$$

Accordingly these ratios may be used to "write down" both the gross and net stock ratios for the subsequent years, up to the disappearance of the initial capital stock.

2.7 Summary of Model

The model used to estimate the capital stock may, therefore, be summarised as follows:

1. We have a series of investment data on purchases and sales of varying kinds of assets distinguished by new and second-hand categories. These series are deflated by the appropriate price indices, and adjustments are made to the second-hand data to bring about equivalence to the "new" purchases.
2. For estimates of the gross stock, investments are retained in the estimating series throughout their life and then retired. For estimates of the "net stock" relative to the gross stock, assets are linearly depreciated to zero over their working life.
3. From estimates of gross and net stocks, and knowledge of the gross fixed capital formation series, measures of capital consumption and net capital formation may be developed.

In order to construct such estimates, data sources relating to purchases and sales, prices, and the length of lifetime of the capital equipment are necessary. In the next chapter we consider such sources for the Irish Republic: also there are certain peculiarities of the series which have to be considered.

Chapter 3

The Perpetual Inventory Model and Irish Data Sources

3.1 Introduction

In the construction of capital stock estimates via the PI method, we have seen that the data requirements are a series of capital expenditures for different types of equipment (inclusive of second-hand purchases and sales); appropriate price deflators, and knowledge of average lives of different types of capital equipment.

For estimation of the capital stock in Ireland, the basic data series on investment expenditures and the capital stock are derived from the Census of Industrial Production (CIP). The first CIP was taken in 1926, the second in 1929, and the third in 1931; thereafter the census was taken annually, but with differing coverage by industry than the preceding studies. Up until 1945 the reports concerned themselves with details of gross output, materials used, net output of salaries and wages, and persons engaged. From 1945 the scope of the census was extended "to include returns of certain supplementary costs of production in addition to salaries, wages, and earnings previously furnished, the value of stocks and work in progress, the value of fixed capital assets at the end of the year, and changes in fixed capital assets during the year". Since 1950 details of fixed capital assets employed were not taken, and in 1953 the industry classification was changed to bring it into conformity with the UN preferred ISIC.

Any estimation of the capital stock based solely on capital expenditure figures, has, therefore, to begin at 1945. Given estimates of the capital stock at year end 1945, and details of annual purchases and expenditures of stock since that date, it, therefore, becomes feasible to calculate the capital stock via the PI method. The details published in the *Statistical Bulletin* are adequate for this task, however, rather more detailed information may be found in the original data sheets of the CSO.[1] These data sheets are wholly compatible with the published data, except that a finer breakdown is given for certain categories of asset.

The treatment of the data therefore falls into three parts; first, determination of the average lifetime of elements of the capital stock, by industrial

---

[1]Kindly made available to the present author by Professor E. Henry of the ESRI.

classification and type of capital equipment; secondly, determination of appropriate price deflators; thirdly, the treatment of the capital expenditure series (inclusive of the initial capital stock) using the average lifetimes and price deflators, by the methods outlined in the preceding chapter. We begin with the problem of estimating the life of capital equipment.

3.2   The Lifetime of Capital Equipment — Methods of Estimation

The length of time for which a particular type of capital equipment is used may depend on a variety of economic and physical factors. The physical factors essentially relate to the capacity of the machine to fulfil with adequate efficiency the task to which it is assigned. As the machine ages, so it may require additional maintenance, suffer prolonged periods of breakdown, until there comes a time when replacement is necessary. The economic factors concerning the replacement of machinery relate to such factors as the output of a machine, the selling price of that output, the price of inputs (including wages), the availability of machines of greater efficiency, and the availability of finance for new investment. Such conditions are likely to change over time as well as to differ between different industries, or different firms in the same industry; thus the "lifetime" of capital may appear as something of a chimera.

The lifetime that appears in PI estimates, therefore, can only constitute an average of the lifetimes of the various types of machinery and equipment that a company has at its disposal at a given moment. What, therefore, are the sources of information from which this average lifetime may be obtained?

(a) A Census or Sample of Assets

One suggestion that might be considered is that a census or sample survey of assets be undertaken. However, the cross section average lifetime thus estimated need not reflect the "longitudinal" estimate of the average life of plant necessary for the PI estimate; and, of course, a sample survey, unless continuing, would not be of great use if the economic factors influencing industry and thus average lifetime change. In the case of Ireland, no records of age of machinery are generally available. However, some fragmentary information on the age structure of the capital stock for certain industries was collected by the Committee on Industrial Organisation.

(b) Use of Average Lifetimes estimated for Other Countries

A second possibility is the use of estimates of average lifetime of plant and machinery for other countries, e.g., the UK or the US. Such estimates were in fact used as a base in Henry's study (1971).

However, the difficulty with relying on estimates for other countries is that the average lifetime reflects the particular economic conditions within those countries, once it is realised that the average lifetime is an economic rather than a technologically determined variable.

(c) Use of Tax Guidelines

In a number of countries the tax authorities prepare guidelines with respect to the depreciation rate at which different types of asset in different industries may be written off for the purpose of claiming tax allowances. Such depreciation rates may be determined with regard to the average lifetime of plant and machinery, and decided in consultation with representatives of the appropriate industry. Such guidelines have, in fact, been prepared by the Revenue Commissioners for Ireland, and published in *Taxation on Industry* (1953).

(d) Use of Depreciation Figures from Company Accounts

Given estimates of depreciation and value of capital employed from the company accounts then it may be possible to derive estimates of the lifetime used in the writing down of plant and equipment.

(e) Combining Investment Expenditures with Independent Information in the Capital Stock

Given independent information on the capital stock, at a particular date and knowledge of investment expenditures prior to that date, then estimates of the lifetime may be possible.

In this study, we shall use method (d); however, since the depreciation charged in company accounts is dependent on the tax structure and the system of investment allowances in operation, we briefly consider the system of depreciation allowances in Ireland for the period which is relevant to our study.

3.3 Taxation and Depreciation Allowances and their Relation to Estimates of the Average Lifetime of Plant and Machinery

In recent years depreciation allowances have come to be one of the tools whereby governments have sought to encourage new investment and modernisation of existing plant and machinery. Ireland is no exception to this rule; consequently the use of the Revenue Commissioners' recent depreciation rules may bear no relation to the actual lifetime of plant and equipment; i.e., the effect of accelerated depreciation allowances. However, the practice at the beginning of the period, 1945-1973 was that depreciation allowances should accurately reflect the "wastage" of capital. The early income tax acts provided that in charging the profits of a trade, a deduction may be allowed for the diminished value by reason of wear and tear during the year of any machinery or plant used for the purposes of the trade. The acts did not prescribe any rates of wear and tear for any class of machinery, but certain rates for the particular types of machinery employed in different trades were followed in actual administration. If a trader was dissatisfied with the annual deduction allowed for wear and tear of machinery, he could have recourse to the Special Commissioners.

Normally, the annual wear and tear deduction was calculated as a percentage of the cost price as diminished year by year by the amount of previous depreciation allowances, i.e., the declining balance method. The asset has, therefore, formally infinite life; however, in such calculations it is usually assumed that there is some cut-off point at which the asset is scrapped. With p, the depreciation rate specified by the Revenue Commissioners, then the time taken to write down an original investment to x per cent of its original value, can be derived as[2]

$$t = \frac{[\log x/100]}{\log (1 - p)} \tag{3.1}$$

Table 3.1: *Depreciation rates and implied lifetimes as determined by the Revenue Commissioners*

	Allowed rates	Implied lifetime (years)
New machinery and plant (other than road vehicles)	10%	22
Other machinery and plant (excluding road vehicles)	No fixed rates. Allowances based on life of assets	
Road vehicles	20%	10
Industrial buildings	2%	114

Source: Taxation on Industry (1953)

In Table 3.1 are given details of the depreciation rates and the length of life implied for such (under the assumption x per cent = 10 per cent), as

---

[2]Let value of investment in year zero be I; then value of investment in year t = $(1 - p)^t I$.
We require, $\frac{(1 - p)^t I}{I}$ = x%; and thus $t = \frac{[\log x/100]}{\log (1-p)}$

specified by the Revenue Commissioners. Whilst these figures are useful as indicators of the magnitude of the average age of types of machinery in different industries, they are of no special use in calculation unless we have the particular industry mix of equipment. This leads us to the second avenue of approach, in so far as we have details on balance sheet depreciation for given years and measures of the capital stock.

3.4 Estimates of Average Lifetime from Balance Sheets of Companies

The equation governing the evolution of the capital stock of a company via the declining balance (or geometric) depreciation method is given by,

$$K(t) = K(t-1) + I(t) - \delta K(t-1) \qquad (3.2)$$

i.e., depreciation is viewed simply as proportional to the size of the capital stock. Thus given $D(t) = \delta K(t-1)$ and $K(t-1)$, an estimate of δ is simply,

$$\delta = D(t) / K(t-1) \qquad (3.3)$$

with the value of δ thus determined, t can be calculated from (3.1).

Data are available on the capital stock distinguished according to (1) plant, machinery, and vehicles, and (2) buildings and land, as measured by book value for the six years, 1945-50. A preliminary estimate of δ may therefore be taken as

$$\delta = \frac{1}{5} \sum_{t=1946}^{1950} \frac{D(t)}{K(t-1)} \qquad (3.4)$$

i.e., as an average of the δs for each of the five years. However, a number of additional points have to be taken into account before a reasonable δ is taken.

(i)   First, consider the problem of inflation. The value of the capital stock represents the book value of assets; might it not be argued, therefore, that these should be brought up to current valuation in determining the depreciation rate? However, both depreciation and the capital stock are in historic cost terms, and if any adjustment is made then it should be made to both. However, when depreciation is exponential, as noted above, the value of depreciation in any given year is independent of the age structure of the capital stock, and consequently both inflation factors are equal.

(ii) The estimates of average lifetime are thus derived for plant and

accordingly, we may consider the use of appropriate indices for each of the cases.

(i)   Passenger Vehicles and Work Vehicles
      The index number for these vehicles was constructed on the basis of the value and volume indices of the gross output of CIP 49, i.e., motor vehicle assembly.

(ii) Plant, Machinery and Other Fixed Assets
      The price index for plant, machinery, and other fixed assets is the average of the indices: Wholesale Price Index for "Imported Producer Goods" and the price index of transportable capital goods for industry. In the case of plant and machinery, it may be expected that imported capital goods play a somewhat larger role in the provision of new capital equipment than motor vehicles domestically produced. Ideally, one may wish for an index of non-exported domestic production of plant and machinery sold, plus a measure of imports; the composite price index being appropriately weighted. However, since such appropriate weights are not available, a simple average of the two price series are taken.

(iii) Buildings and Land
      With respect to the purchase of buildings we propose to use the Wholesale Price Index for Building and Construction published as a sub-sector of the "Capital Goods" Indices. Purchases of land are shown separately in our basic series and we accordingly require an index of land prices. Whilst purchases of plant and machinery, and to a degree, buildings, are to some extent standard commodities, each plot of land is relatively unique, and thus calculation of a price index may be all the harder. The index we propose to use is that compiled by Henry (1971), from the CSO work files, up until 1968; and from that date based on the work of Shanley and Boland (1973).
It should be noted at this point that second-hand purchases and sales were treated as outlined in Section 2.5.

3.7 The UN Gross Fixed Capital Formation Adjustment
A shortcoming of the CIP data is the neglect of the investment of new firms, a point was noted by Nevin (1963): viz., that the CIP data do not include expenditures by new enterprises not yet in production (and hence not making a census return). Such expenditures may include the cost of a new factory and plant, and since this information is not collected for the CIP

Table 3.5: *Price deflators*

	Plant, machinery and other fixed assets	Pass. vehicles and work vehicles	Buildings	Land
1945	0.5711	0.7053	0.450	0.61
1946	0.5865	0.6862	0.556	0.64
1947	0.6515	0.7586	0.648	0.67
1948	0.7145	0.7399	0.703	0.70
1949	0.7170	0.7376	0.706	0.73
1950	0.7345	0.7514	0.732	0.76
1951	0.8104	0.8427	0.785	0.79
1952	0.8978	0.9030	0.873	0.82
1953	0.8780	0.9114	0.8811	0.85
1954	0.8802	0.8955	0.8626	0.88
1955	0.9188	0.8861	0.8837	0.91
1956	0.9587	0.9731	0.9401	0.94
1957	0.9934	0.9794	0.9824	0.97
1958	1.0000	1.0000	1.0000	1.00
1959	1.0044	0.9918	0.9806	1.00
1960	1.0114	1.0027	1.0088	1.05
1961	1.0356	1.0892	1.0493	1.25
1962	1.0544	1.1479	1.1048	1.50
1963	1.0601	1.1746	1.1145	1.75
1964	1.0961	1.2196	1.2000	2.00
1965	1.1155	1.2804	1.2361	2.25
1966	1.1440	1.3459	1.2916	2.50
1967	1.1664	1.4577	1.3400	2.75
1968	1.2260	1.4395	1.3965	3.64
1969	1.2730	1.4405	1.5470	4.99
1970	1.3490	1.5973	1.7210	4.89
1971	1.4430	1.6686	1.9010	5.46
1972	1.5380	1.8234	2.0990	6.24
1973	1.6500	1.8740	2.3820	6.52

Sources: Henry (1971) Appendix 1. CSO Wholesale Price Indices: Plant and Machinery, Buildings and Land

Table 3.6: *UN GFCF deflators*

Year	UN GFCF (1) (£m)	CIP GFCF (2) (£m)	Deflator (3) = (2)/(1)
1946			0.601 (est.)
1947	7.4	4.2	0.57
1948	9.7	5.5	0.57
1949	10.2	6.3	0.62
1950	11.3	7.0	0.62
1951	13.7	7.9	0.57
1952	13.6	8.7	0.64
1953	11.6	9.1	0.79
1954	11.5	9.6	0.84
1955	12.5	10.0	0.80
1956	11.3	8.8	0.78
1957	11.5	10.1	0.88
1958	12.3	7.9	0.64
1959	12.1	10.2	0.85
1960	18.5	13.3	0.72
1961	22.1	19.1	0.86
1962	17.5	23.2	1.00 *
1963	30.5	27.9	0.91
1964	32.8	29.5	0.90
1965	36.8	32.2	0.88
1966	38.8	39.8	1.00 *
1967	41.1	37.6	0.91
1968	49.8	41.7	0.84
1969	62.1	56.1	0.90
1970	72.9	59.6	0.82
1971	84.3	73.0	0.87
1972			0.87 (est)
1973			0.87 (est)

Source: CIP 1947-71

UN Yearbook of National Income Statistics, 1972 and 1973 are set equal to
the 1971 figure due to unavailability of the UN data.

*For explanation of the 1962 and 1966 ratios, see text.

retrospectively, the factor becomes important if one wishes to consider a time series relating, e.g., employment, as given by the CIP to estimates of the capital stock. Thus, when new firms come into production, their employment figures would enter the CIP, but the capital embodied in their new factories is lost. In order to compensate for these omissions we propose to bring about consistency of the CIP estimates for Gross Fixed Capital Formation, with those for GFCF in manufacturing published in the UN Yearbook of National Accounts statistics. Such a method, originally suggested by Nevin, entails an adjustment to all net purchases (in manufacturing) by the UN deflation factors presented in Table 3.6. Column (1) denotes Gross Fixed Capital Formation (GFCF) in manufacturing industry as derived from the UN Yearbook of National Accounts (1974, 1977); whilst column (2) denotes the equivalent figure derived from the CIP. The quotient (2)/(1) is the proportion of UN GFCF accounted for by the CIP. It would, of course, be desirable to have an accurate accounting of "new enterprise" investment, but without such data we have followed the simple expedient of deflating by the series of the quotient (2)/(1); i.e., net purchases of all industries were simply divided through by this third column of Table 3.6. This implies, of course, that the distribution of GFCF as between assets of "new enterprises" remains in the same proportion as for existing firms; such an assumption, it may be suggested, tends to understate investment in buildings and land. We also have the implication that the proportional distribution of "new enterprise" investment as between sectors is the same as that for existing firms; which may cast further doubt on the reasonableness of the assumption. However, although "new enterprises" may be attracted to the faster growing sectors, so also it may be assumed does investment of existing firms, which may make the assumption of equality of proportional distribution of investment across sectors somewhat more palatable.

For two years, 1962 and 1965, UN GFCF was noted as below the amount recorded by the CIP; in such circumstances, rather than reduce the CIP estimates to the UN series, we have simply assumed that the CIP estimates do adequately represent GFCF for those years; hence, for these cases, the deflator is assumed to be unity, irrespective of the UN GFCF estimates. It should be recognised that this approximation exercise is not wholly satisfactory, and it is to be hoped that future inclusion of "start-up" investments in the CIP would obviate the need for future adjustments of this kind.

3.8 Summary of Irish Data Sources

In order to utilise the model outlined in Chapter 2 to estimate the capital stock in Ireland, information on capital expenditures, lifetimes of assets, and indices of price movements are required.

1. The basic data series on investment expenditures and the initial capital stock are derived from the Census of Industrial Production (CIP).

2. Estimations of the average lifetime for components of the capital stock are based on depreciation figures published in the CIP for the years 1945-50 in association with the depreciation rates and implied lifetimes as determined by the Revenue Commissioners.

3. Sales and purchases of investment goods in current value terms are put on a constant price basis (1958 = 100). We have separate information on purchase and sales of passenger and working vehicles, plant and machinery, land, buildings, and other fixed assets. The price indices, apart from vehicles and land, are derived from the appropriate CSO wholesale price indices. The index number for vehicles is constructed on the basis of the value and volume indices for the gross output of CIP 49, i.e., motor vehicle assembly. The price index for land updates Henry's (1971) series from the work of Shanley and Boland (1973).

In addition, the following major adjustments were made to the data:

4. The initial capital stock (1945 or 1950 dependent on industry) was transformed from book value to gross capital stock at replacement cost new, and the associated net capital stock value, according to the procedure outlined in Section 2.6. In order to accomplish this transformation, estimates of the rate of change of prices for the years preceding 1945 or 1950 are required, and price indices derived by Nevin (1963) were utilised.

5. A shortcoming of the CIP data is the neglect of the investment of new firms. The expenditure series were thus adjusted to bring about consistency between the CIP estimates for Gross Fixed Capital Formation (GFCF) with that for GFCF in manufacturing as published for Ireland in the United Nations Yearbook of National Accounts Statistics.

6. Second-hand purchases and sales were treated as outlined in Section 2.5. Thus we assumed that 50 per cent of second-hand purchases and sales were bought or sold halfway through the lifetime of the asset; whilst each remaining 25 per cent were bought or sold a quarter and three-quarter way through the lifetime. The purchase price is assumed to reflect the net capital value of these assets, hence appropriate up-valuation to reflect the gross capital value.

Chapter 4

Estimates of the Capital Stock in Irish Manufacturing Industry

4.1 Introduction

On the basis of the model outlined in Chapter 2, and the Irish data series on investment, prices, and other constitutive elements presented in Chapter 3, we are able to generate estimates of the capital stock for manufacturing industry distinguished by ten major industrial sectors, subdivided into fifty individual industries. In grouping industries by sector, we have used the identical classifications as the Central Statistics Office in relation to the Census of Industrial Production, and therefore the estimates are consistent with all other CSO measures relevant to a particular sector, e.g., measures of output and employment. The estimates for individual industries and sectors are presented either for the years 1945-73, or 1950-73, depending on the availability of data. All estimates refer to the end of the year in question, unless otherwise stated. In addition to measures of the gross and net capital stock, we also have additional measures of gross investment, depreciation, and capital consumption. Both constant and current price estimates for certain categories are presented.

It may be stressed that the estimates which are presented in this chapter are the result of aggregation either over industry, over type of capital good, or both; investment goods were distinguished both according to new and second-hand purchase in compiling the estimates.

4.2 Estimates for Total Manufacturing Industry

In Table 4.1 are presented details of gross and net capital stock estimates for the period 1950-73, along with associated depreciation and capital consumption series. The estimates are presented in constant 1958 prices in £m. The schema follows that suggested in Chapter 2. The first column Gross Fixed Capital Formation (G), essentially constitutes our basic data source, deflated to constant price terms. On the basis of our retirement assumptions, we derive the value of the gross stock that is discarded each year (Column 2), and hence the difference between gross capital formation and discards denotes the change in the value of the gross capital stock (Column 3). The change in the gross stock is then added, for each year, to our base period estimate of the gross capital stock, and so the gross capital stock series (Column 4) is generated.

Table 4.1: *Gross and Net Capital Stock Formation*
All manufacturing industries (constant 1958 prices) £m

Year	Gross fixed capital formation (G)	Gross stock discarded	Change in gross stock	Gross capital stock	Gross fixed capital formation (N)	Capital consumption	Net capital formation	Net capital stock
1950					171.4			107.9
1951	20.6	6.6	14.0	185.4	17.5	6.4	11.1	119.0
1952	17.7	7.9	9.8	195.2	16.0	7.5	8.5	127.5
1953	15.0	6.5	8.5	203.7	14.1	6.8	7.3	134.8
1954	15.5	5.9	9.6	213.3	14.4	7.2	7.2	142.0
1955	16.3	5.6	10.7	224.0	15.0	7.5	7.5	149.5
1956	13.7	6.0	7.7	231.7	12.8	7.7	5.1	154.6
1957	13.5	5.8	7.7	239.4	12.5	8.1	4.4	159.0
1958	19.3	7.4	11.9	251.3	18.0	8.3	9.7	168.7
1959	14.8	6.9	7.9	259.2	13.3	8.8	4.5	173.2
1960	23.3	7.6	15.7	274.9	21.1	9.2	11.9	185.1
1961	24.0	8.1	15.9	290.8	22.5	9.8	12.7	197.8
1962	24.7	7.6	17.1	307.9	23.1	10.5	12.6	210.4
1963	31.9	8.3	23.6	331.5	30.4	11.2	19.2	229.6
1964	33.3	7.5	25.8	357.3	31.5	11.3	20.2	249.8
1965	35.4	10.1	25.3	382.6	33.6	13.7	19.9	269.7
1966	38.6	9.1	29.5	412.1	36.6	13.6	23.0	292.7
1967	40.0	12.0	28.0	440.1	36.9	15.8	21.1	313.8
1968	44.2	10.6	33.6	473.7	41.4	15.7	25.7	339.5
1969	52.8	12.3	40.5	514.2	49.0	18.1	30.9	370.4
1970	57.3	14.2	43.1	557.3	53.2	19.5	33.7	404.1
1971	61.3	15.4	45.9	603.2	57.0	21.1	35.9	440.0
1972	85.0	19.7	65.3	668.5	79.6	25.1	54.5	494.5
1973	70.4	14.8	55.6	724.1	66.0	24.9	41.1	535.6

A similar operation is performed in relation to the generation of the net capital stock. The Gross Fixed Capital Formation (N) (Column 5) differs from Column 1 due to the alternative treatment of second-hand purchases and sales, which has been discussed in Chapter 2. Subtraction from GFCF (N) of capital consumption (Column 6), gives net capital formation (Column 7), which again is added to our base period estimate of the net capital stock, to generate the net capital stock series (Column 8).

A similar table may be presented in terms of current prices, Table 4.2. In the construction of this table, we may note that the Gross Fixed Capital Formation (G and N) is blown up from Table 4.1, by the appropriate price index, as are the Gross and Net Capital Stocks. Columns 3 and 7 are then the respective first differences of the Gross and Net Series, whilst Columns (2) and (7) are simply the difference between Columns 1 and 3; and Columns (5) and (7) and thus a "residual" in the sense that the influence of price changes is lumped into these columns. The influence of price effects on current valuation, can of course be seen in the more recent years with negative values for gross stock discarded and capital consumption; these

Table 4.2: *Gross and Net Capital Stock Formation*
All manufacturing industries (current prices) £m

Year	Gross fixed capital formation (G)	Gross stock discarded	Change in gross stock	Gross capital stock	Gross fixed capital formation (N)	Capital consumption	Net capital formation	Net capital stock
1950				125.9				79.3
1951	16.4	− 6.1	22.5	148.4	14.1	− 1.7	15.8	95.1
1952	15.7	− 8.8	24.5	172.9	14.2	− 3.9	18.1	113.2
1953	13.1	6.2	6.9	179.8	12.4	6.9	5.5	118.7
1954	13.6	7.1	6.5	186.3	12.6	7.2	5.4	124.1
1955	14.7	− 0.6	15.3	201.6	13.5	2.8	10.7	134.8
1956	13.2	− 5.5	18.7	220.3	12.2	− 0.1	12.3	147.1
1957	13.3	− 2.5	15.8	236.1	12.4	2.4	10.0	157.1
1958	19.2	4.1	15.1	251.2	18.0	6.4	11.6	168.7
1959	14.6	8.1	6.5	257.7	13.3	9.9	3.4	172.1
1960	23.6	3.7	19.9	277.6	21.3	6.3	15.0	187.1
1961	25.1	− 1.5	26.6	304.2	23.5	3.8	19.7	206.8
1962	26.6	− 2.9	29.5	333.7	25.0	3.5	21.5	228.3
1963	34.6	5.9	28.7	362.4	32.9	9.6	23.3	251.6
1964	38.2	−10.5	48.7	411.1	35.8	− 0.6	36.4	288.0
1965	41.2	1.2	40.0	451.1	39.2	8.1	31.1	319.1
1966	46.3	− 4.8	51.1	502.2	43.9	5.1	38.8	357.9
1967	49.9	− 0.7	50.6	552.8	46.0	8.3	37.7	395.6
1968	57.9	−12.5	70.4	623.2	54.0	0.2	53.8	449.4
1969	72.4	−27.1	99.5	722.7	67.2	− 9.2	76.4	525.8
1970	84.8	−37.1	121.9	844.6	79.0	−12.2	91.2	617.0
1971	98.4	−44.3	142.7	987.3	91.5	−19.4	110.9	727.9
1972	145.0	−48.7	193.7	1181.0	135.6	−20.0	155.6	883.5
1973	132.2	−82.7	214.9	1395.9	123.5	−38.1	161.6	1045.1

values simply imply that the increase in the nominal value of the stock exceeds gross fixed capital formation even after depreciation or capital consumption is taken into account.

4.3   Estimates by Industrial Sector

The estimates in Tables 4.1 and 4.2 are the summation of estimates for individual industries; the capital stock also being distinguished according to broad categories of capital good, including land, buildings, plant and machinery, and vehicles. In Table 4.3 is provided a breakdown of the gross capital stock estimates according to ten major industrial sectors in constant price terms. The constitutive industries of each of the sectors are defined below in Appendix B. Table 4.4. provides a similar breakdown of the aggregate net capital stock figures; whilst Tables 4.5 and 4.6 provide the corresponding current price estimates. Across sectors, the figures give an indication of the changing structural balance of the Irish manufacturing sector. We may consider the percentage distribution of the capital stock across industries, as in Table 4.7, for the gross and net stock in constant prices. As can be seen, we have a shift away from Sectors I-VI over the period 1953-1973 towards Sectors VII to X, the largest relative shift being away from the food and food processing industries. Both the gross and net figures tell the same story; the gross figures, as noted above, being an indicator of the relative current output potential of the capital stock, whilst the net figures may indicate the relative future potential of the current capital stock.

Table 4.7: *Distribution of capital stock across manufacturing sectors (at constant prices)*

		Gross stock			Net stock		
Year		1953	1963	1973	1953	1963	1973
Sector							
I	Food	31.5	28.7	24.5	31.5	27.8	23.3
II	Drink and Tobacco	14.5	13.9	11.6	14.2	13.4	10.6
III	Textiles	10.7	10.6	10.7	10.8	10.4	10.7
IV	Clothing and footwear	4.2	3.5	2.7	4.1	3.2	2.5
V	Wood	2.9	2.6	2.4	2.9	2.6	2.4
VI	Printing and paper	8.9	8.4	6.4	9.0	8.1	5.8
VII	Chemicals	4.5	5.9	8.3	4.5	6.2	8.7
VIII	Minerals	5.7	5.9	9.4	5.6	5.9	9.7
IX	Metals	12.3	13.9	15.7	13.0	15.2	17.2
X	Miscellaneous	4.8	6.6	8.3	4.6	7.3	9.2
	Total	100.0	100.0	100.0	100.0	100.0	100.0

An alternative method of indicating the changing structure of the capital stock by industry is to note the differential rates of growth between sectors. The rates of growth, together with estimates of gross and net capital formation (relative to gross capital stock) are given in Tables 4.8a and 4.8b, for the period 1953-63, and 1963-73, respectively. As can be seen there was a marked increase in the growth rates of all sectors, as between the two periods. Although, it should be stressed that growth did not proceed smoothly at the indicated growth rates, as will be noted below. The growth rate increased from 5.0 per cent to 8.1 per cent on a yearly basis, with a corresponding spread of rates as between 3.0 per cent for clothing and footwear, and 8.4 per cent miscellaneous manufactures, and between 5.2 per cent for printing and paper to 13.3 per cent minerals. As implied in the preceding discussion, growth rates were the highest in sectors VII-X. As between 1953-63, Gross Capital Formation amounted to £197m. (in 1958 prices), although depreciation amounted to £69m. leading to a value of net capital formation of £128m. over the period, or just £13m. per year.

Table 4.8a: *Gross capital formation: 1953-1963 (constant prices) £'000*

	CIP industry or group	Capital stock end-1953	Gross capital formation	Estimated depreciation	Net capital formation	Capital stock end-1963	Growth rate	
							Continuous	Yearly
I	Food	64314.3	54376.3	23549.1	30827.2	95141.5	0.039	0.040
II	Drink and tobacco	29455.9	24876.4	8132.5	16743.9	46199.8	0.045	0.046
III	Textiles	21775.1	20509.9	7167.6	13342.3	35117.4	0.048	0.049
IV	Clothing and footwear	8599.5	5920.8	3001.9	2918.9	11518.4	0.030	0.030
V	Wood	5891.9	5610.4	2866.6	2743.8	8635.7	0.038	0.039
VI	Printing and paper	17942.0	15219.2	5503.5	9715.7	27657.7	0.043	0.044
VII	Chemicals	9166.9	13690.0	3261.5	10428.5	19595.4	0.076	0.079
VIII	Minerals	11719.7	11925.5	4038.0	7887.5	19607.2	0.051	0.053
IX	Metals	25147.7	28623.3	7571.3	21052.0	46199.7	0.061	0.063
X	Miscellaneous	9736.6	15852.8	3708.2	12144.6	21881.2	0.081	0.084
	Total	203749.6	196604.6	68800.2	127804.4	331554.0	0.049	0.050

Table 4.8b: *Gross capital formation: 1963-1973 (constant prices) £'000*

	CIP industry or group	Capital stock end-1963	Gross capital formation	Estimated depreciation	Net capital formation	Capital stock end-1973	Growth rate	
							Continuous	Yearly
I	Food	95141.5	116524.5	34522.1	82002.4	177143.9	0.062	0.064
II	Drink and tobacco	46199.8	51973.7	14025.9	37947.8	84147.6	0.060	0.062
III	Textiles	35117.4	56759.1	14030.1	42729.0	77846.4	0.080	0.082
IV	Clothing and footwear	11518.4	13760.3	5725.2	8035.1	19553.5	0.053	0.054
V	Wood	8635.7	13912.0	4825.4	9086.6	17722.3	0.072	0.075
VI	Printing and paper	27657.7	28119.7	3719.6	18400.1	46057.8	0.051	0.052
VII	Chemicals	19595.4	47988.4	7772.0	40216.4	59811.8	0.112	0.118
VIII	Minerals	19607.2	56198.2	7459.3	48738.9	68346.1	0.125	0.133
IX	Metals	46199.7	85535.6	17898.0	67637.6	113837.3	0.090	0.094
X	Miscellaneous	21881.2	46856.6	8917.5	37939.1	59820.3	0.101	0.106
	Total	331554.0	517628.1	124895.1	392733.0	724287.0	0.078	0.081

For the period, 1963-73, again in constant prices, gross capital formation amounted to £518m., with depreciation some £125m., leading to net capital formation of some £393m. or close to £40m. per year.

The estimated gross investment (relative to the gross capital stock) is given in Tables 4.9 and 4.10 for plant, machinery and vehicles (in constant prices), and in Tables 4.11 and 4.12 in terms of current prices. The relative stagnation of most industries in terms of level of expenditures on gross investments during the 1950s can be clearly seen in these tables, again, of course, influencing the lower growth rates evidenced in Table 4.8a. As the capital stock expands, larger gross investments are required for any given growth rate, due to the concomitant higher level of retirements from the capital stock.

Chapter 5

Comparison of Capital Stock Estimates with Earlier Studies

5.1 Introduction

It is desirable to check estimates of the capital stock against alternative information; a number of studies of the Irish capital stock exist, therefore in this chapter it is proposed to contrast the results of these studies, and attempt to appraise the reasons for the discrepancies, if any, which exist. The studies which conern us here are those by Nevin (1963), Kennedy (1971), and Henry (1971). The first estimates were undertaken by Nevin, whose analysis was subsequently extended and developed by Kennedy. A new approach was undertaken by Henry.

Before considering existing estimates, we may note, in the light of the previous chapters, certain "all purpose" criticisms of any estimates that may be made, when such estimates are based on the PI method.

First, we may note that a requirement of estimation of the capital stock via PI is knowledge of a time series related to purchases and sales of that asset. If we are interested in the estimation of the stock at a particular date, then data before that date must stretch back at least as long as the life of the oldest asset entering into that stock. When such information is not available (which is usually the case) supplementary information on the magnitude of the capital stock at some date is necessary. The treatment of the figure, due to its large relative magnitude in relation to the net purchase series is of crucial importance, and a source of ready criticisms in relation to assumptions regarding the valuation, depreciation, etc.

A second requirement is the choice of a depreciation function; criticisms may be made that its shape is inappropriate; that the life of the asset is either too long or too short; that the data series utilised is not disaggregated enough by sector, or type of capital good to ensure an accurate choice of the depreciation function.

Thirdly, criticism is sometimes voiced that the capital stock figures derived are not in the desired form required by economic analysts.

5.2 The Study of Nevin

The basic methodology of Nevin's study was as follows. An estimate of the Capital Stock of the Republic, by industry, was derived for the year

1958 independently of the PI method. This figure was derived via a sample of the balance sheet of companies, grossed up so as to give estimates of the fixed assets of all companies engaged in manufacturing. The book values of the assets (at historic cost) were also adjusted upwards to their "insurance valuations", the latter information being available only for a limited number of companies. Nevin took these insurance values as approximating "written down replacement values at current prices", i.e., "net capital stock". Additional estimates were also made of rented capital. Taking this 1958 stock as a basis, Nevin then worked backwards and forwards from 1958, using estimates of net purchases of fixed capital derived from the CIP (adjusted to bring about consistency with National Income estimates of Gross Fixed Capital Formation) to derive a time series of the capital stock. It may therefore be noted that the growth rate of the capital stock as estimated by Nevin is independent of the assumed level of the capital stock in 1958.

The concept of capital that Nevin attempted to measure was undoubtedly the net capital stock; assets being depreciated to zero over the lifetime of the asset.

Kennedy (1971) has provided updated estimates of Nevin's figures for the extended period (1946-1966), as against Nevin's original period (1947-1959). Henry (1971) also reworked the Nevin series for the period (1954-1969), under Nevin's assumptions.

5.3   The Study of Kennedy

Kennedy's (1971) study, besides extending the period for which capital stock estimates are available also made certain modifications to Nevin's estimation process. Kennedy noted certain errors in Nevin's analysis; thus Nevin appeared to have misclassified the hosiery and leather industries in relation to industry groups, which led to an overstatement of the average level of assets in "textiles" and "miscellaneous", and an understatement in clothing. Kennedy also notes that "the estimates of the average lives of plant, etc. in the metals and minerals group appears to have been incorrectly calculated."

Kennedy thus recalculates the estimates on the basis of revised lifetime figures, however, as Kennedy notes "the revisions in the estimates of capital stock here involve only marginal differences from Nevin's figures in all groups except clothing".

5.4   The Study of Henry

Henry's study differed substantially from that of Nevin and Kennedy, in that estimates of the capital stock were derived recursively from a PI method moving forward from a given base year. Henry's analysis begins with criticism of Nevin's (and by implication Kennedy's) method of estimation. Among the criticisms were the following:

(i)   It is doubtful whether Nevin's assumption that "insurance valuations" approximates "written down replacement value at current prices", i.e., whether the net capital stock value in fact is correct; this error, if present, would set the whole Nevin series at the "wrong" level.

(ii) Since Nevin was attempting to measure net capital stock, such a concept "is not particularly useful for some applications of the results", e.g., Nevin's analysis of productivity.

(iii) The average life of plant and machinery assumed by Nevin was in certain cases, excessive. This can be seen to be a result of the method of derivation of average life and relied on estimates of the capital stock at a given date; too high an estimate of this stock leads to longer estimates of average life.

(iv) Nevin insufficiently disaggregated the assets leading to incorrect assumptions regarding average lives.

With regard to Henry's study, as noted Henry estimates the capital stock moving forward from a given base year. The measure of the capital stock which Henry aimed at was essentially that of Gross Stock, which Henry terms "equivalent new". Assets were linearly depreciated to 80 per cent or 85 per cent of their original values (in constant price terms) over their lifetimes; whilst the lifetime of assets varies as between industries. Unlike Nevin's analysis, both the level and the trend of the capital stock are dependent on assumptions regarding the size of the initial stock; since the initial stock is depreciated over subsequent years.

Criticisms of Henry's method are the following:

(i)   It may be argued that doubtful factors are applied to second-hand purchases and sales to derive "equivalent-new" estimates. Similarly, it has been argued (Jefferson (1971), Slattery (1975)) that the grossing-up factor applied to the initial capital stock to derive "equivalent new" estimates is too low. These factors are introduced by Henry *a priori* into the analysis without consideration of their economic determinants.

(ii) Depreciation factors applied to the Initial Capital Stock are incorrect. The initial capital stock figures were depreciated by Henry over half the average working lifetime. Thus if vehicles had an average life of eight years, the entire capital stock would be written off in four years. Thus the problem of the most recently bought elements of the initial capital stock are ignored, and this may lead to quite absurd results; e.g., four years into the capital stock figures and within the space of one year, the stock of vehicles may be decimated.

(iii) Henry does not consider the elements of Gross Fixed Capital Formation not reported by (future) CIP respondents. Nevin pointed out that the CIP data does not include expenditures by new enterprises not yet in production (and hence not making a census return); such expenditure may include the cost of a new factory and plant; neither is this information collected by the CSO retrospectively. This factor becomes important if one wishes to consider a time series relating, e.g., employment, as given by the CIP to estimates of the capital stock. When new firms come into production then their employment figures enter the CIP, but the capital embodied in their new factories is lost. Henry argues that the "CIP figures for GFCF are reliable enough to be compared with the Gross Output and Employment figures, all for CIP respondents." The greater the influx of new firms then the more doubtful the veracity of this assumption.

5.5   Comparison of Results

Let us now turn to a comparison of the results of Nevin-Kennedy (N-K), Henry (H), and the gross and net capital series (GSV and NSV) presented in Chapter 4. In Tables 5.1 and 5.2 are presented Kennedy's revision of Nevin's estimates, and Henry's estimates, distinguished by manufacturing sector. In Table 5.3 we present the comparison for all manufacturing industry, and in Graphs 5.1-5.11 are plotted the estimates of the four different measures for the years 1945-73 (dependent on data availability), again distinguished by sector.

GRAPHS

Note: In Graphs 5.1—5.11, the series GSV and NSV refer respectively to the gross and net stock figures derived from Tables 4.13 and 4.14 and are *end-year* estimates. The series NK refers to Kennedy's revision of Nevin's capital estimates and are derived from Table 5.1, whilst the H series refers to the Henry capital estimates derived from Table 5.2; both the NK and H series are *mid-year* estimates. For definition of GSV' and NSV' see p. 72 of text.

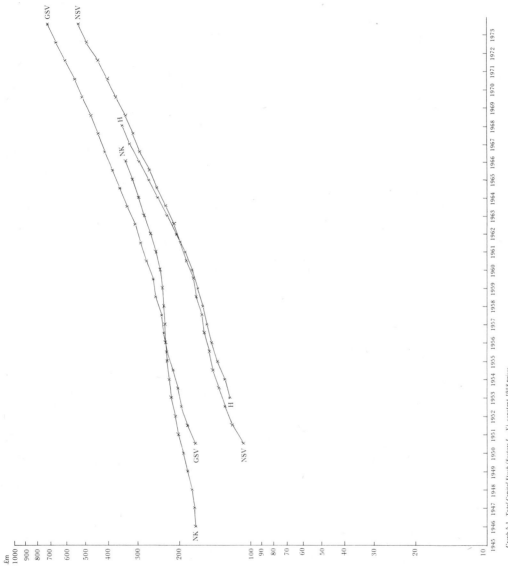

Graph 5.1 *Total Capital Stock (Sectors I – X), constant 1958 prices.*

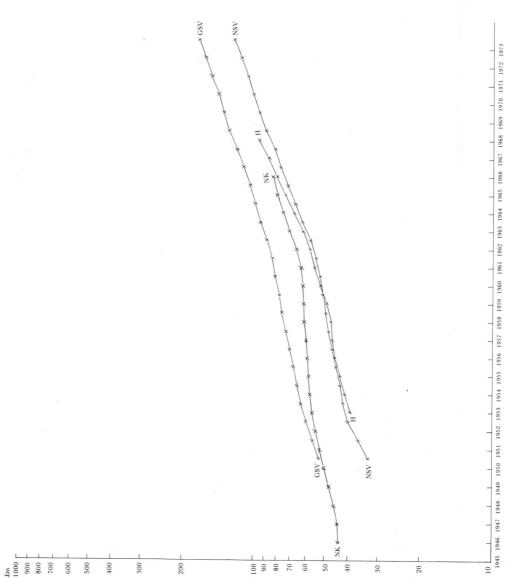

Graph 5.2 *Capital Stock Estimates, Sector I (Food), constant 1958 prices.*

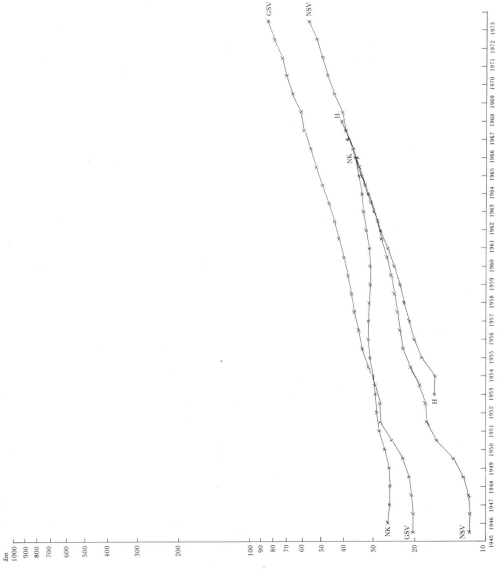

Graph 5.3 *Capital Stock Estimates, Sector H (Drink and Tobacco), constant 1958 prices.*

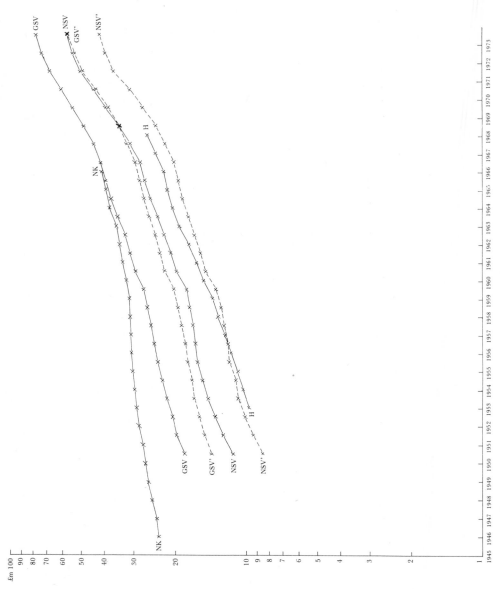

Graph 5.4 *Capital Stock Estimates, Sector III (Textiles), constant 1958 prices.*

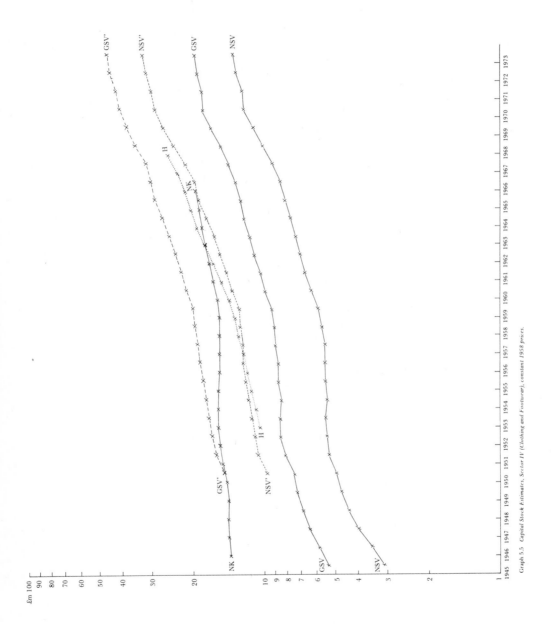

Graph 5.5 *Capital Stock Estimates, Sector IV (Clothing and Footwear), constant 1958 prices.*

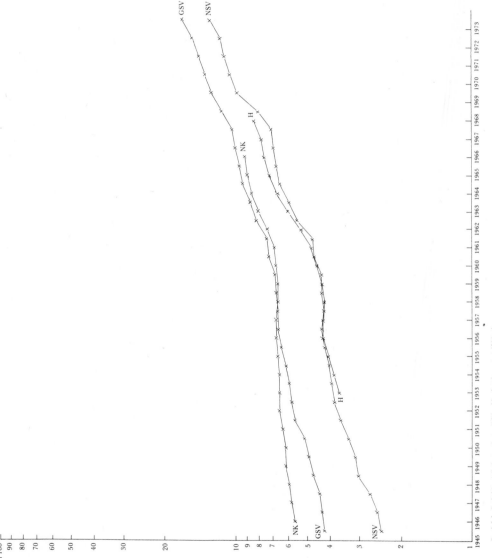

Graph 5.6 Capital Stock Estimates, Sector V (Wood Products), constant 1958 prices.

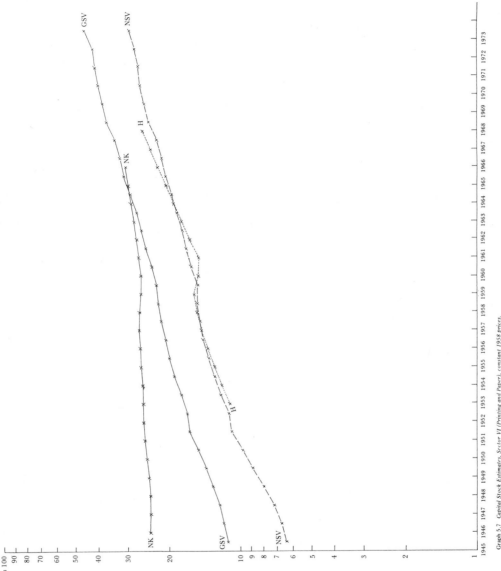

Graph 5.7 *Capital Stock Estimates, Sector VI (Printing and Paper), constant 1958 prices.*

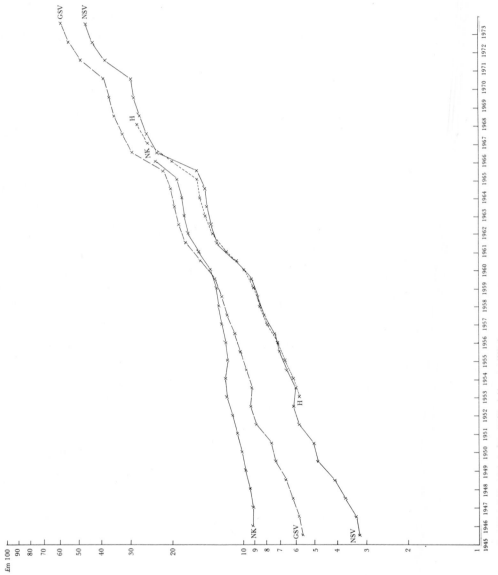

Graph 5.8 *Capital Stock Estimates, Sector VII (Chemicals), constant 1958 prices.*

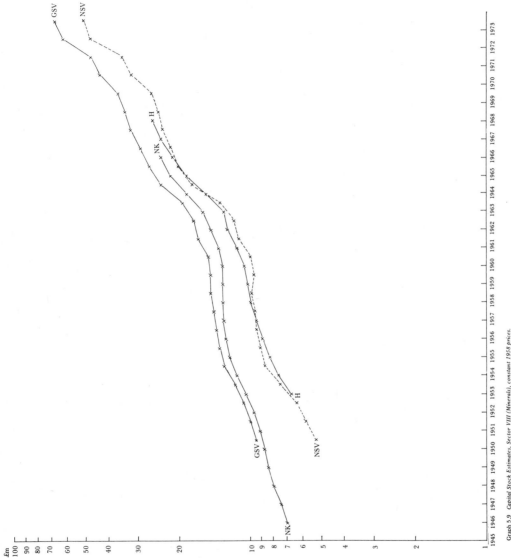

Graph 5.9 *Capital Stock Estimates, Sector VIII (Minerals), constant 1958 prices.*

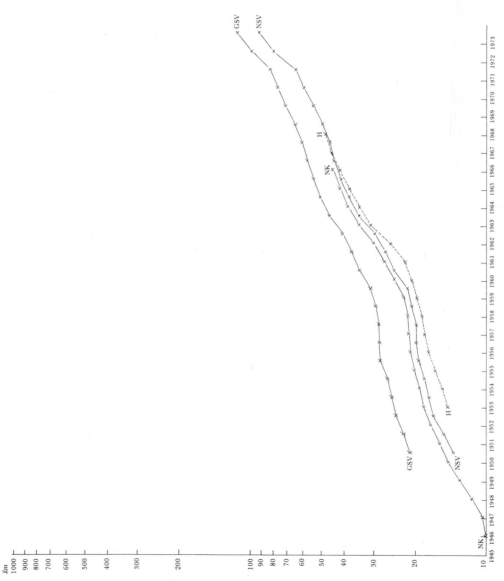

Graph 5.10 *Capital Stock Estimates, Sector IX (Metals), constant 1958 prices.*

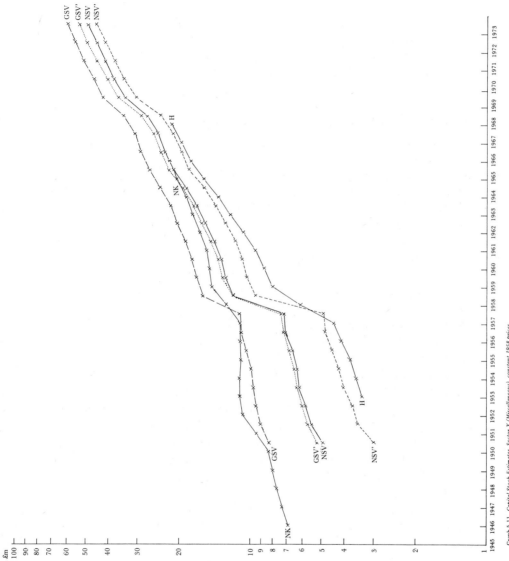

Graph 5.11 *Capital Stock Estimates, Sector X (Miscellaneous), constant 1958 prices.*

A second point to note is the difference in the absolute levels of the series, particularly H and N-K. The H measure, is a representation closer to the "Gross Stock" definition of capital; whilst N-K, as defined by Nevin and Kennedy, is viewed as a net stock measure. In any consistent framework, the net figure should not exceed the gross figure. Is there any way in which the estimates can be reconciled? Evidently, the disjunction in the levels of N-K and H may be explained either by the fact that Nevin pitched his estimates of the 1958 stock too high to reasonably approximate the net capital stock level, or that Henry estimated the initial capital in 1950 or 1945 at too low a level; or, naturally, some combination of the two. The divergence in trends may also be partly explained by the influence òf the initial stock of capital. In the N-K figures, the assumed capital stock does not influence the trend, as noted above. The other three series can be viewed as being composed of two elements. The post-1950 (or 1945) capital stock, i.e., the amount of capital purchased since that date, and the depreciating 1950 (or 1945) stock. Due to the magnitude of the initial stock, this dominates the initial years of the H, GSV and NSV series; the higher valuation, or alternative depreciation assumptions, critically affect both the level and the trend. Under conditions of constant growth of purchases of investment goods, all series would be expected to converge eventually with regard to their growth paths, but not with respect to their absolute levels.

In constructing the industrial sectors, i.e., aggregating the individual industries, we have followed the CIP convention, as followed, for example, by Kennedy. The comparison with the N-K estimates is exact: however, the classification adopted by Henry differs in certain respects, as given in Table 5.4. Consequently, in Sectors III, IV, and X, we have also constructed graphs according to the Henry classification (GSV' and NSV'), in order for exact comparability with the Henry (H) series in these sectors.

We have noted that H represents "equivalent new", a gross measure of the capital stock (a = 0.8); NSV a net stock measure (a = 0); and GSV a gross stock measure (a = 1) where "a" is a parameter defined in relation to the linear depreciation function (Eq. (5.1)); H and NSV, GSV also have widely differing assumptions regarding life of assets; yet the growth rates of all are remarkably similar. The identity of growth rates can in fact be explained as a consequence of the linear depreciation function, and constant growth in net purchases of assets.

Thus, with lifetime of assets given by (T − L) we have

$$F(t, T) = 1 - (1 - a) \left[\frac{T - t}{T - L} \right] \qquad (5.1)$$

as defining the efficiency of vintage t (as measured by output) in relation to that of the most recent capital of vintage T.

Table 5.4: *Comparison of industrial classifications*

Industry N-K and V classification	Henry classification
Textiles	
Woollen and worsted (excluding clothing)	,,
Linen and cotton spinnings, weaving and manufactures	,,
Jute, canvas, rayon etc.	,,
Hosiery	(Hosiery excluded)
Manufacture of made-up textiles	,,
Clothing	
Boot and shoe	,,
Clothing: men's and boys'	,,
shirtmaking	,,
women's and girls'	,,
miscellaneous clothing	,,
(Hosiery excluded)	Hosiery
	Fellmongery, tanning and dressing of leather
(excluded)	Manufactures of leather and leather substitutes
Miscellaneous	
Fellmongery, tanning and dressing of leather	
Manufactures of leather and leather substitutes except footwear and other weaving apparel	(excluded)
Miscellaneous manufacturing industries	

If such were the case then the ratio of values of the capital stock under alternative assumptions regarding the choice of "a" can be shown to be

$$\frac{V(T, a)}{V(T, 1)} = 1 - \frac{(1-a)}{(T-L)} \frac{1}{g} - \frac{(1-a)}{(1 - c^{g}(T-L))} = \beta \quad (5.2)$$

and hence,

$$\frac{d}{dT} \log \left\{ V(T, a) \right\} = \frac{d}{dT} \log \left\{ V(T, 1) \right\} \quad (5.3)$$

i.e., the growth rate is invariant to the choice of a. We can also show that,

$$\frac{V(T, 1, X_2)}{V(T, 1, X_1)} = \frac{(1 - e^{-gX_2})}{(1 - e^{-gX_1})} = \xi \qquad (5.4)$$

where X_1 and X_2 are differing lives of the same asset; hence since

$$V(T, a, X_2) = \beta_2 \ V(T, 1, X_2); V(T, a, X_1) = \beta_1 \ V(T, 1, X_1)$$

Then,

$$\frac{V(T, a, X_2)}{V(T, a, X_1)} = \frac{\beta_2}{\beta_1} \xi \qquad (5.5)$$

i.e., the growth rate is also invariant with respect to the lifetime of assets. An implication of this result is that in a constant growth economy we need not run into any error by using the growth of net capital, say, in a productivity study, when gross capital would be more appropriate.

5.6 Summary

In this chapter we have considered previous studies of the capital stock of Irish manufacturing industry, and have contrasted their results with those of the present study. The studies of Nevin (1963), Kennedy (1971), and Henry (1971) have been subject to a number of criticisms, major points being:

(i)   The assertion of incorrect treatment of the initial, or baseline, capital stock. Thus the Nevin (and Kennedy) estimates have been criticised on the grounds that insurance estimates used do not reflect written down replacement value. In Henry's study it has been argued that the grossing factors applied to the initial capital stock to derive "equivalent new" estimates were too low.

(ii)   The assumed average lifetimes of certain assets may be incorrect; in the case of Nevin's estimates it has been suggested that since Nevin's estimates of lifetime depended upon initial estimates of the size of the capital stock, if the latter was set at too high a level as suggested above, then so would the lifetimes generated be somewhat excessive.

(iii) In so far as the CIP has neglected the investment of new "start-up" firms, then so would the capital stock be understated, as it has been argued occurs in Henry's study.

We should, however, note that such criticisms, in particular concerning the size of the initial capital stock and lifetimes entering the depreciation function, are almost certain to be a matter for debate, and are an inevitable consequence of utilising the PI method for estimation of the capital stock, the present study being no exception.

With regard to comparison of the series, we may note:

(a) The similarity in the trends of the series of Henry and those of the present study, although these measures were constructed under quite different assumptions regarding depreciation, lifetime of assets, and valuation of the initial capital stock. The closeness of the trends suggests that the adjustments to the data have been multiplicative with regard to the end effect, hence leading to a linear displacement on logarithmic paper as in Graphs 5.1-5.11.

(b) All the studies agree that a structural shift to a higher trend occurred in the period 1959-61, although the trends of the Henry series and those of the present paper appear rather more pronounced than in the Nevin-Kennedy studies. The divergence in trends may be partly explained by the influence of the initial stock of capital and the subsequent effect of its depreciation on future net capital accumulation.

Chapter 6

The Development of Capital Stock Estimates

6.1 Introduction

With regard to the capital stock estimates we may note two main avenues for future improvement and research. On the one hand, we may accept the basic PI model as outlined in previous chapters, and consider improvements in the basic input of the Irish data series. On the other hand, one may question more fundamentally the PI model, in particular, the rigidity of its assumptions regarding the determination of replacement investment. We have emphasised the interrelationship between the PI model and the theory of investment behaviour, and it is likely that in this direction major developments in the future modelling of the capital stock are likely to appear. The alternative to PI models, namely, a census or sample survey of assets would not appear to be a major practical alternative. In many cases capital estimates are required within a time series framework, and since such surveys have not taken place, as has been the case in Ireland, then there is no viable alternative to the PI method. However, such surveys may be of importance in the construction of capital benchmarks.

Overshadowing the enterprise of the construction of capital stock measures is, of course, the question of the usefulness of the exercise, given recent attacks on the concept of capital by Robinson (1969), and others. It should be apparent that the estimates of capital provided by the PI method are certainly a far cry from the theorists ideal definition of capital, e.g., as a factor employed in production. Although we do not consider the circularity arguments of Robinson (1969), Harcourt (1972) of particular importance in this connection (e.g., note the discussion in Hahn (1972)); the general problem of aggregation, both temporally, over commodities, and over industries, is of supreme importance. We consider below a possible rationalisation of the use of capital stock estimates, in terms of distributed lag models; the general problems of aggregation are beyond the scope of this paper.

Finally, we come to the problem of verifying or disproving the capital stocks estimated by the PI method. As should by now be apparent, the PI "estimation" procedure generates no suitable diagnostics against which the accuracy of the estimates may be judged. We consider briefly the possibilities regarding the development of such tests.

6.2   The Rigidity of PI Capital Estimates

We have noted in previous chapters the crucial role in the estimation of the capital stock played by the depreciation function, and hence, in view of the assumption of "sudden-death" and "straight line" depreciation, the importance of the average lifetime assumed for the capital good in question. We have no evidence, within Ireland, on the correctness, or otherwise, of our particular choice of depreciation function, and alternatives may also be thought to be appropriate, e.g., the "quasi-logistic", the "normal", or the "Winfrey" patterns of depreciation. Furthermore, the lifetimes estimated were based on the period 1945-50 and the depreciation practices then in use, which may be wholly inappropriate for the modern period. Furthermore, we have no information in our estimates concerning quality change in the constituents of the capital stock, in so far as such change is not reflected in the price changes of the capital goods in question.

However, over and above such questions concerning quality change and choice of appropriate depreciation function, we have a peculiar form of rigidity in the investment function, relating to the distribution of investment expenditures in any given year as between "expansion" and "replacement" investment. "Replacement" investment is always some fixed proportion of investments in previous years, and indeed, under the "one-horse shay" or "sudden death" assumption, is equal to total investment which occurred "n" years previously, where "n" is the appropriate average life of the asset. However, the rate at which assets are discarded or sold is dependent on a number of factors, besides customary depletion or material exhaustion of the good. Whilst material exhaustion may be a technical factor independent of economic conditions (given constancy of utilisation) facing a company at a particular time, other factors which influence the replacement decision are not. It is, indeed, doubtful whether capital goods are worked to physical death; indeed, maintenance and replacement parts may prolong the physical life of an asset almost indefinitely. However, it may become unprofitable, given current input costs to continue to use an existing asset; or alternatively, higher profits may be earned with a replacement. Thus there may exist quite an appreciable length of time in which the company may choose to replace a capital good, and the precise date may depend primarily on economic factors, such as, e.g., the state of demand for the company's product, the availability of finance, tax incentives provided by the government, or the price and expected prices of other inputs such as labour services and raw materials. Since such influences may be presumed to change over time, and in so far as they predominate in the choice of the date of replacement, so a capital stock model in which replacement schedules are fixed may generate incorrect estimates of the capital stock.

Given this basic weakness of existing PI models, are there any methods by which the fault may be rectified? One possibility would be to attempt to incorporate explicitly an economic theory of replacement investment, which in any case may be needed for any large scale model of the economy. The existing equation for replacement investment in the PI model as a distributed lag function of past investment totals could be changed to one in which we have explicit dependence on variables thought to influence the replacement investment decision. A start on the construction of such a theory has been made by Feldstein and Foot (1971), and Feldstein and Rothschild (1975); however this theory is insufficiently advanced to consider incorporation within the PI model at present; such theories also inevitably require a much wider data base in relation to individual industries than is currently available in Ireland.

The rigidities of the PI model consequent on the generation of the replacement investment series by a mechanical depreciation rule is, of course, not the only criticism of the PI method, and a recent summary of such criticisms may be found in Ward (1976). However, such criticisms that Ward does put forward, apart from those relating to the depreciation function, are not we feel, specific to the PI method, but generally arise whenever "prices" and "quantities" arise in empirical work. We have already remarked on the difficulties which may arise with regard to the appropriate choice of price deflators, the problem of quality change and technical progress; in addition problems arise concerning the "utilisation" of capital, and concerning the treatment of "circulating" capital or inventories, which are not included in the PI estimates. Such problems, although mentioned by Ward, are not strictly criticisms of the PI methodology, although perhaps it should be stressed that PI does not concern itself with the wider aspects of capital employed in a firm or industry, excluding the aforementioned circulating capital, and indeed the major aspects of financial capital.

6.3 Capital Stock as a "Constructed" Variable

Given the above criticisms to the derivation of capital stock estimates via the PI method, one may legitimately inquire as to whether the estimates that are produced are of any practical use?

It should be remembered that the estimates are indeed simply transformations of three basic sources of data; a series of purchases (and sales) of investment goods in current price terms; a set of price indices; and initial estimates of the capital stock for some base year, i.e.,

$$K_t = F(I_t, I_{t-1}, \ldots, I_{t-k}; P_t, P_{t-1}, \ldots, P_{t-k}; K_{t-k}; \lambda_1 \lambda_2, \ldots, \lambda_m)$$

where $[\lambda_1, \lambda_2, \ldots\ldots, \lambda_m]$ is some set of parameters referring to the assumptions regarding the depreciation profile of the capital goods over their lifetime. Given a relationship, with unknown K_t, then it should be possible in any quantitative analysis involving the capital stock to substitute out for that variable in terms of past real values of investment. In many cases such a procedure is preferable, since it reflects the fact that the capital stock is generally not homogeneous with regard to its temporal components.

Why then is such a procedure not generally followed, since it would appear to obviate the need for a capital stock estimate, only an investment series? In certain studies a capital stock series has indeed been dispensed with; e.g., Dhrymes (1969), the time profile of the capital stock is presumed to influence output (and the demand for other factor services) via incorporation into the estimation procedure levels of current and past investment expenditures. However, whilst such a procedure may best encompass the fact that capital goods of different vintages embody different levels of technical advance, and thus may contribute differentially to output or production, there is an obvious statistical drawback.

Using investment data rather than capital stock in any econometric modelling exercise involves losing k degrees of freedom in the estimation procedure, where k is the number of lags required to encompass all investment contributions. Since k may be expected to be large, dependent on the economic circumstances mentioned above, then so we have a decrease in the number of effective observations that may be used. The PI method in this statistical context therefore may be simply viewed as one way around this df problem. Thus we may "construct" a particular variable "K_t" in exactly an analogous manner to the "arithmetic lag" procedure suggested by Fisher (1937), the "inverted V lag" suggested by Deleeuw (1962), or the Almon lag structure, Almon (1965). Further discussion of these and other procedures concerning lag structures may be found in Maddala (1977).

The "Capital Stock" variable may indeed be seen as a special case of a general economic model in which the *cumulation* of a particular variable over time influences current economic actions. The interpretation of the PI "capital" stock as a "constructed" variable in the statistical sense, may allow us to avoid a number of criticisms usually attached to a capital measure; i.e., we explicitly view it as an imperfect variable reflecting a given lag and weighting structure over past investment values and price indices.

Finally, we come to the problem of the verification of the PI model, i.e., how can we determine that the capital stock estimates thus generated adequately reflect the capital stocks available to industry. It is apparent that the simple cross checking against alternative estimates, e.g., as we have done in relation to the studies of Nevin-Kennedy, and Henry, can provide little or no satisfaction in this respect, since each of the studies is based on its own assumptions regarding lifetime of capital, depreciation function, etc. Even should a census of assets be available for comparison, quite different values may be obtained as against the PI estimates for the same date unless consistent procedures with respect to valuation were followed.

It would thus appear that the only method of accepting or rejecting the PI estimates is by direct tests of the assumptions that constitute the model. One particular test that may be suggested is the so-called "echo effect" consequent on the particular mortality distribution assumed. As noted by Jorgenson (1971), an extreme form of the "echo effect" is associated with a periodic mortality distribution, resulting in a periodic distribution of replacements and periodic cycles of replacement investment. A form of echo effect was tested for by Meyer and Kuh (1957) for individual firms. As reported by Jorgenson, Meyer and Kuh's results are "not out of line with the null hypothesis that the echo effect plays no role in the determination of investment for individual firms" (p. 1140), if such were the case, then this would cast doubt on the fixity of depreciation functions assumed by the PI model. Evidently further work on this topic is warranted, possibly using the newer methods of time series analysis that have been discovered since Meyer and Kuh's 1957 analysis (e.g., Granger and Newbold (1977)).

APPENDICES

Appendix A
Gross and Net Capital Stock by Type of Capital Good and Industrial Sector

In this Appendix we present details of Gross and Net Capital Stock Measure distinguished by type of capital good (at constant prices), for all manufacturing industries (Table A.1) and for the ten major industrial sectors (Tables A.2—A.11).

Appendix B
Alternative Industrial Classifications

Table A.1: *All industries (constant 1958 prices) £'000*

Year	Gross stock				Net stock			
	Total	Vehicles	Plant and machinery	Buildings and land	Total	Vehicles	Plant and machinery	Buildings and land
1950	171345.4	14268.7	73603.6	83473.1	107925.7	8277.1	45096.4	54552.2
1951	185370.0	14752.4	79898.9	90718.7	119114.2	8729.5	50958.6	59426.1
1952	195154.8	14982.7	86217.0	93955.1	127587.6	8786.5	56471.4	62329.7
1953	203749.5	15127.2	93319.2	95303.1	134699.0	8563.1	62603.2	63532.7
1954	213328.6	15471.0	99679.4	98178.2	141992.5	8688.5	67579.3	65724.7
1955	223749.9	15704.3	106422.6	101623.0	149513.2	8794.1	72368.0	68351.1
1956	231516.6	16042.9	112151.7	103322.0	154500.2	8644.7	76277.3	69578.2
1957	239287.8	15994.7	117605.8	105687.3	161140.8	8445.8	79466.4	73228.6
1958	251325.7	15815.4	125971.7	109538.6	168590.0	8785.9	85293.6	74510.5
1959	259264.2	15924.0	131651.7	111688.5	173290.3	9056.7	88394.8	75838.8
1960	274890.8	16117.4	141577.1	117196.3	185131.3	9578.4	95457.5	80095.4
1961	290828.4	16389.6	152914.7	121524.1	197646.1	10066.7	103734.7	83844.7
1962	307837.3	16799.0	163824.6	127213.7	210375.0	10303.0	111354.3	88717.7
1963	331554.4	17803.1	180656.2	133095.1	229683.2	10837.9	124937.8	93907.5
1964	357398.6	18529.0	197411.4	141458.2	249704.5	11376.7	137701.9	100625.9
1965	382638.4	19120.8	215193.8	148323.8	269825.1	11863.9	151076.8	106884.4
1966	412048.6	20046.9	235975.0	156026.7	292712.9	12167.4	166952.8	113592.7
1967	440028.5	20595.5	253775.2	-165657.8	313934.1	12251.3	179779.3	121903.5
1968	473796.1	22267.6	277906.4	173622.1	339501.2	13819.7	196284.9	129396.6
1969	514292.5	25224.6	303057.8	186010.1	370573.5	15984.0	214666.8	139922.7
1970	557352.2	27383.3	331414.2	198554.7	404139.0	17803.8	235249.2	151086.0
1971	603043.9	30918.1	361950.0	210175.8	439891.2	20942.0	256282.2	162667.0
1972	668549.6	36401.0	407820.6	224328.0	494609.0	25109.4	292950.1	176549.5
1973	724287.2	40191.8	442952.8	241142.6	535689.6	27235.6	317529.5	190924.5

Table A.2: I Food (constant prices) £'000

Year	Gross stock				Net stock			
	Total	Vehicles	Plant and machinery	Buildings and land	Total	Vehicles	Plant and machinery	Buildings and land
1950	53889.2	5583.7	21412.7	26892.8	33342.0	3259.7	12844.6	17237.7
1951	57104.3	5976.9	23115.0	28012.5	36508.1	3619.0	14573.6	18315.5
1952	61687.4	6147.9	25906.7	29632.7	40364.3	3773.0	16980.5	19610.8
1953	64314.3	6288.5	27856.6	30169.2	42364.3	3785.3	18538.5	20040.5
1954	66415.7	6449.2	29099.7	30866.8	43607.9	3794.8	19263.7	20549.3
1955	69171.6	6614.6	30698.4	31858.7	45503.2	3872.1	20333.9	21297.2
1956	71758.8	6847.7	32406.4	32504.7	47065.8	3835.8	21418.9	21811.1
1957	74891.6	7173.9	34129.8	33587.9	48966.1	3939.5	22445.8	22580.7
1958	77478.9	7403.4	35814.5	34261.2	50641.4	4173.1	23355.4	23112.9
1959	79418.3	7516.3	37045.1	34857.1	51689.0	4243.3	23919.1	23526.5
1960	82100.0	7555.1	38496.2	36048.8	53443.6	4390.2	24586.0	24467.4
1961	85031.0	7545.3	40519.6	36966.2	55713.0	4499.1	25916.3	25297.6
1962	89014.3	7652.1	42808.3	38554.1	58742.9	4618.7	27445.8	26678.4
1963	95141.5	7932.5	46717.7	40491.4	63927.3	4739.3	30786.6	28401.4
1964	100545.9	8267.4	50084.2	42194.5	68094.3	4891.0	33384.3	29819.1
1965	106924.4	8421.3	54180.5	44322.7	73181.8	5036.8	36285.6	31859.5
1966	113649.4	8668.0	58149.7	46831.9	78313.4	5122.1	39143.7	34047.7
1967	120574.5	8691.7	62612.1	49270.8	83614.0	5118.0	42132.7	36363.4
1968	130050.7	9327.9	68804.7	51918.2	91266.1	5730.2	46497.5	39038.5
1969	137763.6	10030.9	73688.5	54044.2	96432.5	6154.8	49586.6	40691.3
1970	146480.9	10587.7	79393.7	56499.6	102855.9	6687.4	53360.7	42807.9
1971	155592.7	11323.3	84453.4	59816.0	109130.6	7157.3	56398.5	45574.9
1972	164575.6	11905.8	91357.1	61312.8	116493.6	7591.4	61232.0	47670.4
1973	177143.9	12770.5	96295.0	68078.6	124638.9	8041.6	63149.3	53448.1

Table A.3: II Drink and Tobacco (constant prices) £'000

Year	Gross stock				Net stock			
	Total	Vehicles	Plant and machinery	Buildings and land	Total	Vehicles	Plant and machinery	Buildings and land
1945	20446.9	1265.5	7154.1	12027.3	11726.9	632.8	3577.0	7517.1
1946	20331.4	1194.8	7092.7	12043.8	11608.3	583.3	3502.1	7522.9
1947	20560.9	1152.3	7305.7	12103.0	11836.7	573.7	3729.8	7533.1
1948	21198.6	1274.9	7741.0	12182.6	12426.8	718.1	4144.1	7564.6
1949	22517.9	1362.3	8815.3	12340.4	13677.2	806.4	5198.7	7672.1
1950	25124.4	1416.3	10620.6	13087.5	16101.7	869.4	6906.2	8326.1
1951	28016.4	1533.8	11557.1	14925.0	17782.9	1007.6	7683.4	9091.9
1952	28011.3	1578.7	12155.2	14277.3	17964.3	1013.8	8172.6	8777.8
1953	29455.9	1610.1	13675.7	14170.1	19203.2	964.4	9573.7	8665.0
1954	31641.0	1637.8	15252.5	14750.7	21018.1	951.1	10908.0	9159.0
1955	33598.7	1673.9	16943.4	14981.5	22602.9	949.0	12315.2	9338.7
1956	34760.1	1751.8	17968.3	15039.9	23221.5	914.9	12965.4	9341.1
1957	35998.1	1787.3	19025.3	15185.6	23814.3	859.1	13566.9	9388.3
1958	37059.5	1652.4	20263.6	15143.5	24459.5	825.5	14314.5	9319.5
1959	38202.8	1575.8	21302.4	15324.5	24965.8	808.5	14750.2	9407.0
1960	39946.4	1544.7	22765.6	15636.0	26180.7	836.4	15671.6	9672.7
1961	41782.2	1453.5	24482.0	15846.7	27510.5	877.7	16821.5	9811.4
1962	43699.1	1382.2	25944.1	16372.8	28889.7	861.6	17734.1	10294.1
1963	46199.8	1599.1	27514.4	17086.3	30748.7	1021.5	18632.7	11094.5
1964	49304.2	1796.5	28684.5	18823.1	32964.2	1181.9	19159.4	12622.9
1965	52557.1	1968.8	30884.9	19703.4	35259.5	1330.9	20563.1	13365.5
1966	55166.8	2135.9	32905.3	20125.6	36886.2	1390.2	21877.1	13619.0
1967	59665.8	2252.3	35832.6	21581.0	39502.8	1368.1	23501.9	14632.8
1968	61676.5	2506.0	38312.9	20857.7	40919.5	1577.3	24755.8	14586.4
1969	66538.7	2882.2	41042.2	22614.3	44204.6	1847.0	26339.9	16017.6
1970	70734.7	3132.6	44417.9	23184.1	47040.8	2047.0	28288.8	16705.0
1971	73906.8	3484.9	47474.6	22947.3	49513.8	2278.1	29900.8	17335.0
1972	78999.9	3832.9	50701.3	24465.8	52837.0	2448.7	31842.0	18546.3
1973	84147.6	4285.9	54150.9	25710.8	56882.2	2790.0	34312.8	19779.5

Table A.4: III Textiles (constant prices) £'000

Year	Gross stock				Net stock			
	Total	Vehicles	Plant and machinery	Buildings and land	Total	Vehicles	Plant and machinery	Buildings and land
1950	18251.4	976.3	9427.1	7848.0	11390.2	538.4	5622.8	5229.0
1951	19727.5	946.7	10416.4	8364.4	12640.4	724.9	6519.8	5595.7
1952	20634.3	937.6	11080.6	8616.1	13628.7	509.3	7241.4	5878.0
1953	21775.1	927.9	11951.3	8895.9	14494.6	481.1	7949.0	6064.4
1954	22782.6	904.9	12728.6	9149.0	15285.6	461.3	8514.9	6309.4
1955	23794.4	903.6	13373.0	9517.9	16019.9	468.1	8882.6	6669.3
1956	24555.1	903.1	13992.7	9659.3	16381.5	465.0	9191.3	6725.2
1957	25332.7	868.5	14582.1	9882.1	16766.0	430.0	9453.9	6882.1
1958	26233.0	835.3	15302.8	10094.8	17301.6	431.7	9838.8	7031.1
1959	27219.4	781.1	16089.7	10348.6	17915.7	423.5	10272.9	7219.2
1960	29607.2	780.4	17975.2	10851.7	19878.5	473.9	11803.0	7601.5
1961	31090.7	813.5	19131.3	11145.9	20855.3	508.1	12488.5	7858.7
1962	32838.3	844.9	20359.2	11634.2	22209.9	532.6	13342.7	8334.6
1963	35117.4	881.7	22064.9	12170.8	23768.3	550.9	14426.2	8791.2
1964	37569.9	910.4	23870.4	12789.0	25526.2	563.6	15696.0	9266.5
1965	39768.6	920.3	25614.4	13233.9	27191.1	575.5	16937.8	9677.8
1966	41376.8	976.8	26880.2	13519.8	28190.6	616.5	17659.1	9915.0
1967	44524.4	1031.9	28821.5	14671.0	31120.0	641.5	19505.4	10973.1
1968	49043.9	1154.5	32316.5	15572.9	34744.5	759.3	22185.0	11800.2
1969	54547.3	1350.0	35692.7	17504.6	39336.2	898.1	24848.4	13589.7
1970	60757.8	1594.4	40222.6	18940.8	44500.8	1097.5	28560.3	14843.1
1971	68155.4	1994.3	46258.4	19902.8	50356.9	1399.4	33172.2	15785.3
1972	73913.5	2134.9	50868.3	20910.4	54638.2	1499.2	36479.3	16659.7
1973	77846.4	2259.5	54201.3	21385.6	57188.4	1559.5	38560.5	17068.4

Table A.5: IV Clothing and Footwear (constant prices) £'000

Year	Gross stock				Net stock			
	Total	Vehicles	Plant and machinery	Buildings and land	Total	Vehicles	Plant and machinery	Buildings and land
1945	5438.4	654.0	1595.3	3189.1	3117.8	327.0	797.7	1993.2
1946	5919.1	643.9	1810.5	3464.7	3455.0	331.0	927.0	2197.0
1947	6477.5	661.2	2001.3	3815.1	4001.4	369.3	1128.0	2504.1
1948	6883.0	685.5	2145.6	4051.9	4358.0	410.1	1274.3	2673.6
1949	7267.9	710.1	2446.4	4111.5	4725.6	438.3	1539.8	2747.5
1950	7531.0	756.7	2645.9	4128.4	4946.6	464.9	1706.2	2775.5
1951	8169.6	792.3	2795.8	4581.5	5287.3	473.0	1826.7	2987.7
1952	8575.2	794.7	2877.0	4903.5	5423.9	460.9	1870.1	3092.9
1953	8599.5	791.9	2944.6	4863.0	5459.7	440.9	1961.9	3057.0
1954	8485.1	775.8	3012.1	4697.2	5383.0	414.5	2014.2	2954.2
1955	8765.8	780.2	3110.3	4875.3	5493.7	414.5	2058.6	3020.6
1956	8774.3	800.6	3179.0	4794.7	5458.1	409.3	2092.9	2955.9
1957	8969.1	760.2	3298.2	4910.6	5542.9	381.5	2154.4	3007.0
1958	9146.5	730.2	3457.5	4958.8	5718.6	394.4	2263.7	3060.4
1959	9349.7	688.3	3667.6	4993.8	5857.0	402.3	2395.4	3059.4
1960	9986.3	676.0	3951.1	5359.2	6314.8	422.2	2588.8	3303.7
1961	10417.0	686.4	4295.8	5434.8	6650.9	435.8	2856.8	3358.4
1962	10952.6	720.6	4617.7	5614.2	7012.4	442.1	3092.7	3477.6
1963	11518.4	749.7	4944.6	5824.1	7346.5	447.4	3310.4	3588.7
1964	12083.8	763.1	5362.8	5957.8	7741.8	442.0	3629.2	3670.6
1965	12597.0	752.5	5717.3	6127.2	8098.8	443.8	3861.4	3793.6
1966	13180.8	779.6	6080.8	6320.5	8524.7	449.3	4096.9	3978.5
1967	14243.7	813.3	6552.6	6877.8	9231.4	463.5	4422.5	4345.4
1968	15340.7	886.1	6974.6	7479.9	10074.2	519.3	4687.9	4867.1
1969	16765.9	970.7	7777.0	8018.2	11214.8	607.4	5313.3	5294.0
1970	17968.2	1070.7	8410.2	8487.2	12096.9	697.8	5775.1	5624.1
1971	18267.8	1044.8	8857.8	8365.1	12429.0	694.2	6029.4	5705.4
1972	19135.4	1106.0	9433.6	8595.7	13143.4	732.5	6437.3	5973.6
1973	19553.5	1199.3	9821.4	8532.7	13544.1	788.4	6705.3	6050.4

Table A.6: *V Wood (constant prices) £'000*

Year	Gross stock				Net stock			
	Total	Vehicles	Plant and machinery	Buildings and land	Total	Vehicles	Plant and machinery	Buildings and land
1945	4197.2	557.9	1037.7	2601.6	2323.8	279.0	518.8	1626.0
1946	4252.4	531.5	1085.8	2635.1	2496.1	282.4	560.8	1652.9
1947	4446.0	545.6	1178.5	2721.8	2703.9	332.6	637.5	1733.8
1948	4742.2	624.4	1275.6	2842.3	2936.1	399.8	746.6	1839.8
1949	4907.9	689.9	1342.3	2875.7	3095.0	446.1	799.7	1849.2
1950	5080.9	717.5	1430.4	2933.0	3289.6	481.8	925.9	1881.8
1951	5579.3	825.7	1694.0	3059.6	3634.3	548.4	1126.6	1959.2
1952	5793.1	883.9	1799.2	3109.9	3807.4	547.8	1234.6	2025.1
1953	5891.9	914.1	1865.8	3111.9	3870.5	542.7	1281.9	2045.8
1954	6095.9	964.2	1953.9	3177.8	3992.1	567.7	1348.2	2076.2
1955	6396.3	1031.6	2156.1	3208.6	4188.6	588.7	1453.2	2146.8
1956	6600.9	1072.1	2173.3	3355.6	4268.1	571.2	1448.2	2248.7
1957	6611.4	1022.3	2194.4	3394.7	4244.6	530.9	1441.5	2272.1
1958	6721.3	980.8	2296.9	3443.6	4272.6	523.9	1456.0	2292.7
1959	6789.6	988.0	2326.7	3474.9	4288.1	541.0	1445.0	2302.1
1960	7171.2	991.0	2575.8	3604.4	4622.9	562.2	1630.1	2430.6
1961	7292.7	983.5	2662.9	3646.3	4727.3	571.7	1715.7	2439.9
1962	8128.2	994.1	3217.9	3916.2	5457.3	553.4	2210.7	2693.2
1963	8635.7	1030.7	3467.2	4137.9	5877.8	586.3	2390.2	2901.3
1964	9308.8	1027.7	3921.0	4360.0	6476.5	613.5	2766.9	3096.1
1965	9631.1	1031.8	4075.0	4524.2	6738.9	623.0	2857.6	3258.3
1966	9962.8	1040.3	4289.8	4632.8	6895.9	601.9	2970.4	3323.6.
1967	10217.9	1068.7	4539.3	4609.8	7048.6	602.1	3103.7	3342.8
1968	11380.9	1266.8	4934.3	5179.7	7967.0	746.7	3413.6	3806.8
1969	13593.7	1876.7	5940.1	5776.9	9828.2	1196.8	4279.2	4352.1
1970	14448.4	1795.3	6546.5	6106.7	10455.5	1167.9	4656.7	4630.9
1971	15325.1	1913.9	7065.2	6345.9	11078.3	1264.7	4960.8	4852.8
1972	16226.0	2050.9	7461.4	6713.8	11564.3	1279.8	5167.8	5116.7
1973	17722.3	2231.1	8102.3	7388.9	12681.9	1408.7	5615.5	5657.7

Table A.7: VI Printing and Paper (constant prices) £'000

Year	Gross stock				Net stock			
	Total	Vehicles	Plant and machinery	Buildings and land	Total	Vehicles	Plant and machinery	Buildings and land
1945	11403.6	466.5	5676.1	5261.0	6359.4	233.3	2838.9	3288.1
1946	11824.3	482.8	5719.5	5622.0	6725.8	260.5	2880.5	3584.9
1947	12343.5	493.5	6042.3	5807.7	7199.2	289.9	3178.9	3730.5
1948	13146.0	544.1	6659.6	5942.2	7950.9	342.8	3752.5	3855.7
1949	14013.0	556.7	7322.4	6133.9	8863.5	356.8	4508.7	3998.0
1950	15068.1	602.1	8100.9	6365.0	9776.6	389.7	5188.9	4198.0
1951	16461.1	645.6	8825.6	6989.9	10867.0	410.3	5833.9	4622.9
1952	16924.0	686.7	9319.4	6917.9	11240.7	415.0	6209.4	4616.3
1953	17942.0	714.2	10056.7	7171.1	12133.9	412.8	6862.4	4858.6
1954	19135.5	754.5	10745.7	7635.3	12907.0	439.0	7400.8	5067.2
1955	19892.4	787.9	11522.2	7582.3	13555.1	448.0	8064.3	5042.8
1956	20763.7	805.3	12228.1	7730.3	14285.6	465.4	8668.5	5151.8
1957	21688.2	783.2	13157.9	7747.1	14868.3	446.0	9293.9	5128.4
1958	22283.2	769.1	13726.4	7787.7	15157.3	460.8	9577.0	5119.5
1959	22564.0	829.6	13858.5	7875.9	15237.2	509.4	9551.1	5176.8
1960	23805.3	847.6	14858.9	8098.8	16082.2	531.7	10216.1	5334.4
1961	25212.7	891.3	15907.5	8413.9	17000.6	572.5	10830.9	5597.2
1962	26340.7	949.4	16756.3	8635.0	17602.7	574.7	11240.4	5787.6
1963	27657.7	1021.2	17506.0	9130.6	18498.9	605.8	11716.2	6176.8
1964	29519.1	1020.9	19080.3	9417.9	19735.5	616.3	12744.3	6374.9
1965	31216.2	1045.1	20363.9	9807.2	20837.7	630.9	13516.6	6690.2
1966	32508.2	1072.0	21360.0	10076.1	21594.7	646.9	14011.0	6936.8
1967	34256.0	1131.2	22573.3	10551.5	22792.6	679.7	14772.1	7340.8
1968	37057.2	1239.7	24599.4	11218.1	24772.7	772.5	16149.2	7851.0
1969	38746.4	1258.3	26043.5	11444.6	25720.2	786.5	16872.8	8060.9
1970	40425.8	1265.8	27090.7	12069.3	26708.5	788.3	17367.1	8553.1
1971	41454.2	1231.9	28098.9	12123.5	27250.7	766.4	17744.5	8739.9
1972	42630.3	1259.0	28564.1	12807.1	28349.4	778.3	18163.6	9407.5
1973	46057.8	1311.2	31238.9	13507.7	30916.7	872.0	20004.3	10040.4

Table A.8: *VII Chemicals (constant prices) £'000*

Year	Gross stock				Net stock			
	Total	Vehicles	Plant and machinery	Buildings and land	Total	Vehicles	Plant and machinery	Buildings and land
1945	5602.2	555.1	2039.5	3007.6	3177.0	277.5	1019.8	1879.8
1946	5780.8	548.8	2107.1	3124.1	3332.9	277.9	1074.3	1980.7
1947	6192.5	546.4	2263.4	3382.8	3677.3	292.6	1220.2	2164.5
1948	6567.6	572.6	2486.2	3508.8	4108.5	325.9	1455.8	2326.8
1949	7272.6	593.2	2880.6	3798.8	4781.9	346.8	1836.0	2599.1
1950	7580.3	627.4	3053.6	3899.3	5009.9	376.0	1963.1	2670.8
1951	8792.7	633.3	3473.1	4686.3	5834.4	375.3	2381.3	3077.8
1952	9264.5	652.7	3723.0	4888.8	6080.5	383.3	2559.5	3137.7
1953	9166.9	663.2	3854.7	4649.0	6035.1	380.1	2658.3	2996.6
1954	9652.0	677.6	4188.5	4786.0	6458.3	394.5	2943.6	3210.2
1955	10288.1	722.4	4475.6	5090.0	6992.0	434.3	3179.8	3377.9
1956	10898.0	774.6	4865.5	5258.0	7431.7	444.0	3508.2	3479.4
1957	11763.0	777.8	5308.7	5676.5	8232.7	459.4	3845.1	3928.3
1958	12303.5	736.8	5588.3	5978.4	8677.9	497.7	4011.0	4169.2
1959	13097.9	832.1	5986.0	6279.8	9228.3	570.9	4312.6	4344.8
1960	15127.7	937.2	7045.9	7144.6	10775.1	649.7	5190.1	4935.2
1961	17517.4	1056.4	8297.8	8163.2	12888.9	724.7	6272.8	5891.3
1962	18759.8	1132.8	9082.3	8544.6	13730.2	744.6	6795.5	6190.1
1963	19595.4	1133.8	9576.2	8885.5	14197.8	732.3	7024.7	6440.8
1964	20290.4	1215.8	9998.5	9076.1	14570.4	782.2	7239.0	6549.2
1965	21909.6	1356.1	11120.3	9433.2	15805.8	870.3	8076.0	6859.5
1966	29720.3	1446.1	17228.2	11046.0	23213.5	891.7	13927.6	8394.2
1967	32871.8	1496.4	19477.2	11898.2	25898.1	925.5	15654.2	9318.4
1968	35430.0	1609.9	21446.0	12374.1	27739.0	1068.8	17021.8	9648.3
1969	37337.5	1810.6	22764.0	12762.8	29006.3	1220.8	17876.5	9908.9
1970	39224.0	1946.2	24906.0	13181.8	30003.2	1314.0	18472.2	10217.0
1971	49069.1	3615.9	29831.1	15622.1	38875.6	3101.3	23160.3	12614.0
1972	54989.2	5078.7	33796.4	16114.1	43760.4	4203.7	26283.3	13273.4
1973	59811.8	5633.4	36968.6	17209.7	46641.3	4298.9	28258.9	14083.4

Table A.9: *VIII Minerals (constant prices) £'000*

Year	Gross stock				Net stock			
	Total	Vehicles	Plant and machinery	Buildings and land	Total	Vehicles	Plant and machinery	Buildings and land
1950	9483.4	1277.4	3553.8	4652.2	5323.2	638.7	1776.9	2907.6
1951	9972.9	1215.6	3877.7	4879.6	5820.6	590.7	2109.8	3120.1
1952	10670.3	1157.7	4109.4	5403.2	6449.7	562.4	2334.0	3553.3
1953	11719.7	1095.2	5008.7	5615.8	7497.1	502.8	3214.7	3779.7
1954	13020.7	1138.7	6037.2	5844.9	8732.4	558.9	4193.6	3979.9
1955	13550.7	1050.1	6287.2	6213.4	9085.4	517.1	4330.7	4237.7
1956	14005.4	990.9	6683.5	6331.0	9436.3	480.1	4620.8	4335.4
1957	14432.4	959.2	6939.4	6533.8	9643.6	456.6	4722.7	4464.3
1958	14810.1	924.4	7231.7	6654.0	9868.0	442.4	4858.3	4567.2
1959	14796.6	869.4	7230.5	6696.7	9746.9	432.6	4734.7	4579.7
1960	15122.1	804.2	7483.4	6834.5	9966.4	440.2	4843.3	4683.0
1961	16657.3	839.6	8758.9	7058.9	11271.9	483.4	5922.2	4866.3
1962	17375.8	822.8	9284.8	7268.2	11759.3	502.0	6222.4	5034.9
1963	19607.2	954.0	11065.8	7587.4	13649.9	587.1	7749.8	5312.9
1964	24243.3	969.1	14885.7	8389.5	17861.8	641.4	11175.8	6044.5
1965	27106.4	988.9	17233.3	8884.2	20161.5	654.4	13023.8	6483.3
1966	29707.0	1073.7	19052.1	9581.3	22016.3	698.9	14202.3	7115.1
1967	32503.6	1170.8	20907.9	10424.8	23810.3	716.7	15246.8	7846.7
1968	34407.8	1272.3	22079.0	11056.4	24816.3	765.5	15675.1	8375.6
1969	36921.3	1261.0	23758.3	11902.0	26460.9	811.3	16537.2	9112.3
1970	44118.0	1726.3	27222.1	15169.7	32411.6	1179.8	19019.8	12212.0
1971	47999.7	1906.1	29320.8	16772.9	35241.4	1295.8	20299.4	13646.2
1972	63374.7	3492.5	40892.9	18989.3	48728.2	2707.7	30307.3	15713.2
1973	68346.1	3882.0	43396.3	21067.9	51800.5	2829.0	31515.7	17455.8

Table A.10: IX Metals (constant prices) £'000

Year	Gross stock				Net stock			
	Total	Vehicles	Plant and machinery	Buildings and land	Total	Vehicles	Plant and machinery	Buildings and land
1950	21034.2	1422.5	10397.1	9214.7	13880.6	758.0	6611.3	6511.3
1951	22536.8	1319.0	10754.5	10463.3	15190.9	703.7	6928.8	7558.4
1952	24235.7	1284.6	11621.4	11329.7	16787.2	664.8	7669.4	8453.0
1953	25147.7	1300.7	12202.9	11644.0	17482.5	642.9	8106.1	8733.5
1954	26179.6	1375.8	12558.6	12245.2	18318.2	727.5	8377.1	9213.6
1955	27950.8	1353.5	13505.2	13092.0	19429.0	727.1	8909.9	9792.1
1956	28523.4	1338.1	13939.8	13245.5	19858.8	714.2	9223.7	9920.9
1957	28554.4	1172.1	14079.4	13302.8	19848.7	636.0	9268.2	9944.4
1958	29475.6	1154.2	14712.0	13609.4	20597.6	726.4	9738.8	10132.3
1959	30980.6	1257.1	15769.2	13954.3	21629.0	801.3	10463.9	10363.8
1960	34470.7	1361.0	17603.2	15506.5	24618.6	883.2	12048.7	11686.7
1961	37037.5	1480.2	19249.7	16357.5	26864.0	959.2	13450.5	12454.3
1962	40465.6	1619.7	21182.0	17663.1	29509.6	1006.4	14997.7	13505.5
1963	46199.7	1731.6	26074.5	18393.6	34856.9	1049.2	19643.7	14164.0
1964	50441.7	1693.0	28364.3	20384.5	38080.2	1067.3	21476.2	15536.7
1965	53994.3	1763.8	30865.0	21365.5	41138.0	1106.9	23507.8	16523.4
1966	57797.3	1895.2	33420.3	22481.8	44017.5	1119.7	25461.8	17435.9
1967	60306.9	1943.9	35661.3	23801.8	46174.0	1117.1	26602.2	18454.8
1968	64944.9	1874.8	37906.1	25164.0	49715.1	1172.7	28998.7	19543.7
1969	70064.2	2169.1	40853.4	27041.8	54124.3	1409.1	31437.8	21277.4
1970	76768.8	2465.8	45134.7	29168.3	59822.6	1647.8	35072.3	23102.5
1971	82301.0	2595.7	48545.1	31160.3	64350.2	1794.2	37632.3	24923.8
1972	99221.1	3558.3	58976.5	36686.5	79906.4	2577.3	47122.4	30206.9
1973	113837.3	4487.9	69911.1	39438.4	92176.1	3257.5	56546.7	32372.0

Table A.11: X Miscellaneous (constant prices) £'000

Year	Gross stock				Net stock			
	Total	Vehicles	Plant and machinery	Buildings and land	Total	Vehicles	Plant and machinery	Buildings and land
1950	8302.5	888.8	2961.5	4452.2	4865.4	500.5	1550.5	2814.4
1951	9009.7	863.5	3389.7	4756.6	5548.2	476.6	1974.7	3096.9
1952	9359.3	858.2	3625.1	4876.0	5840.8	456.2	2199.9	3184.6
1953	9736.6	821.4	3902.2	5013.1	6158.3	410.1	2456.7	3291.6
1954	9920.5	792.5	4102.6	5025.3	6290.9	379.2	2615.2	3295.7
1955	10340.0	785.5	4351.2	5203.3	6643.0	375.2	2839.8	3428.0
1956	10876.8	758.7	4715.1	5403.0	7092.9	344.8	3139.4	3608.7
1957	11055.0	690.2	4898.6	5466.2	7213.8	306.8	3274.0	5633.0
1958	15814.1	628.8	7578.0	7607.2	11895.8	310.0	5880.1	5705.7
1959	16845.2	586.3	8376.0	7882.9	12733.4	323.9	6549.9	5859.5
1960	17573.8	620.2	8821.8	8131.8	13248.7	388.7	6879.8	5980.2
1961	18739.8	639.9	9609.2	8490.7	14163.6	434.5	7459.5	6269.6
1962	20262.7	680.4	10571.1	9011.3	15460.5	466.9	8272.3	6721.3
1963	21881.2	768.8	11724.0	9387.5	16811.4	518.1	9257.3	7035.9
1964	24091.7	865.1	13160.7	10065.8	18653.7	577.5	10430.8	7645.4
1965	26933.7	872.2	15139.2	10922.3	21411.8	591.4	12447.1	8373.3
1966	28978.8	959.3	16608.6	11410.9	23060.0	630.2	13602.9	8826.9
1967	30934.3	995.3	17898.4	12041.6	24742.2	619.1	14837.8	9285.3
1968	34443.6	1129.6	20512.9	12801.1	27486.7	707.4	16900.3	9879.0
1969	42014.0	1615.1	25498.1	14900.7	34245.8	1052.2	21575.1	11613.5
1970	46426.1	1798.5	28880.5	15747.2	38242.0	1176.3	24676.2	12390.4
1971	50972.0	1807.3	32044.7	17119.9	41664.3	1190.6	26984.0	13489.7
1972	55483.4	1982.0	35769.0	17732.5	45187.7	1290.8	29915.1	13981.8
1973	59820.3	2131.0	38867.0	18822.3	49159.3	1390.0	32800.5	14968.8

Appendix B

Alternative Industrial Classifications

Classification in Use Since 1953	Classification in Use Prior to 1953
I Food	I Food
Bacon Factories	Bacon Curing
Creamery butter, cheese, condensed milk, chocolate crumb, ice cream and other edible milk products	Butter, cheese, condensed milk and margarine
Butter blending, margarine and compound cooking fats	
Grain milling and crucial feeding stuffs:	Grain milling and crucial feeding stuffs:
(a) Flour and wheatmeal	(a) Flour and wheatmeal
(b) Other milling products and animal feeding stuffs	(b) Other milling products and animal feeding stuffs
Bread, biscuits and flour confectionery	Bread, flour, confectionery and biscuits
Manufacturing and refining of sugar	Sugar
Manufacture of cocoa, chocolate and sugar confectionery	Sugar confectionery, jam-making, preserved vegetables etc.
Canning of fruit and vegetables and manufacture of preserves, jams, jellies etc.	
Miscellaneous food preparation	
Slaughtering, preparation and preserving of meat other than by bacon factories	Component of "Miscellaneous Industries"
Canning and preserving of fish	

Classification in Use Since 1953	*Classification in Use Prior to 1953*
II Drink and Tobacco	
Distilling	Distilling
Malting	Malting
Brewing	Brewing
Aerated and mineral waters	Aerated and mineral waters
Tobacco	Tobacco
III Textiles	
Woollen and Worsted	Woollen and Worsted
Linen and cotton spinning, weaving and manufactures	
Jute, canvas, rayon, nylon, cordage and miscellaneous textile manufactures	Linen, cotton, jute, canvas and rayon
Manufacture of made-up textile goods (except apparel)	
Hosiery	Hosiery
IV Clothing and Footwear	
Boot and Shoe (wholesale factories)	Boot and Shoe (wholesale factories)
Clothing (wholesale factories)	Clothing (wholesale factories)
Men's and boys'	Men's and boys'
Shirtmaking	Shirtmaking
Women's and girls'	Women's and girls'
Miscellaneous	Miscellaneous
V Wood Products	
Manufacture of wood and cork except furniture	Timber
Manufacture of furniture and fittings	Wood furniture and upholstery
Brushes and Brooms	Brushes and Brooms

Classification in Use Since 1953	Classification in Use Prior to 1953
VI Paper and Printing	
Manufacture of paper and paper products	Papermaking and manufactured stationery
Printing, Publishing and allied trade	Printing, publishing, bookbinding and engraving
VII Chemicals	
Fertilisers	Fertilisers
Oils, paints, inks and polishes	Chemicals, drugs, oils, paints and polishes
Chemicals and drugs	
Soap, detergents and candles	Soap and candles
VIII Minerals	
Glass and glassware, pottery, clay and earthenware	Bricks, pottery, glass, cement and momumental masonry
Structural clay products, asbestos goods, plaster, gypsum and concrete products, slate and dressed stone, cement	
IX Metal	
Metal trades (and machinery and transport equipment)	Metal
Manufacture and assembly of machinery (except elec. equipment)	Engineering and implements
Manufacture of electrical machinery apparatus and appliances	
Ship and boat building and repairing	Ship and boat building and repairing

Classification in Use Since 1953	*Classification in Use Prior to 1953*
Manufacture of railroad equipment	
Assembly, construction and repair of vehicles other than mechanically propelled road and land vehicles	Assembly, construction and repair of vehicles
Assembly, construction and repair of mechanically propelled road and land vehicles	

X   Miscellaneous

Fellmongery, tanning and dressing of leather	Fellmongery and leather
Manufacture of leather and leather substitutes	
*Slaughtering, preparation and preserving of meat other than by bacon factories	Miscellaneous Industries
*Canning and preserving of fish	
Miscellaneous manufacturing industries	

*since 1953 moved to Sector I Food.

REFERENCES

ALMON, S., 1965. "The Distributed Lag Between Capital Appropriation and Net Expenditures", *Econometrica*.

CENTRAL STATISTICS OFFICE, 1945-77. *Irish Statistical Bulletin*, various vols.

COEN, R.M., 1968. "Effects of Tax Policy on Investment in Education", *American Economic Review*, Proceedings, Vol. 58, No. 2, pp. 200-211.

COEN, R.M., 1975. "Investment Behavior, the Measurement of Depreciation, and Tax Policy", *American Economic Review*, Vol. 65, No. 1, pp. 59-74.

DEAN, G., 1964. "The Stock of Fixed Capital in the UK in 1961", *Journal of the Royal Statistical Society*, Series A, Vol. 127, Part 3, pp. 327-351.

DeLEEUW, F., 1962. "The Demand for Capital Goods by Manufacturers: A Study of Quarterly Time Series", *Econometrica*.

DHRYMES, P.J., 1969. "A Model of Short-Run Labor Adjustment", in J.S. Duesenberry *et al.* (eds.) *The Brookings Model: Some Further Results*, Amsterdam: North-Holland.

EVANS, M.K., 1967. "A Study of Industry Investment Decisions", *Review of Economics and Statistics*, Vol. 49, No. 2, pp. 151-164.

FELDSTEIN, M.S. and D.K. FOOT, 1971. "The Other Half of Gross Investment: Replacement and Modernization Expenditures", *Review of Economics and Statistics*, Vol. 53, No. 1, pp. 49-58.

FELDSTEIN, M.S. and M. ROTHSCHILD, 1975. "Toward an Economic Theory of Replacement Investment", *Review of Economics and Statistics*.

FISHER, I., 1937. "Note on a Short-Cut Method for Calculating Distributed Lags", *International Statistical Institute Bulletin*, pp. 323-327.

GEARY, P.T., B.M. WALSH and J. COPELAND, 1975. "The Cost of Capital to Irish Industry", *Economic and Social Review*, Vol. 6, No. 3, pp. 299-311.

GLASS, C.J., 1971. "Factor Substitution and Demand for Labour in the Northern Ireland Engineering Industry", *Journal of the Statistical and Social Inquiry of Ireland*, Vol. XXII, Part IV, pp. 156-185.

GRANGER, C.W.J. and P. NEWBOLD, 1977. *Forecasting Economic Time Series*, New York: Academic Press.

GROES, N., 1976. "Measurement of Capital in Denmark", *Review of Income and Wealth*, Series 22, No. 3, pp. 271-286.

HAHN, F.H., 1972. *The Share of Wages in the National Income*, London: Weidenfeld and Nicolson.

HARCOURT, G.C., 1972. *Some Cambridge Controversies in the Theory of Capital*, Cambridge: Cambridge University Press.

HENRY, E.W., 1971. "Estimation of Capital Stock in Irish Industry, 1953-68", *Journal of the Statistical and Social Inquiry Society of Ireland*, Vol. XXII, Part IV, pp. 1-26.

HIBBERT, J., T.J. GRIFFIN and R.L. WALKER, 1975. "Development of Capital Stock Estimates for the United Kingdom", paper read to the 14th General Conference of the IARIW, Helsinki.

JEFFERSON, C.W., 1968. *A Method of Estimating the Stock of Capital in Northern Ireland Manufacturing Industry: Limitations and Applications,* Dublin: ESRI, Paper No. 44.

JEFFERSON, C.W., 1971. Discussion of the Henry (1971) paper, *Journal of the Statistical and Social Inquiry Society of Ireland*, Vol. XXII, Part IV.

JORGENSON, D.W., 1963. "Capital Theory and Investment Behavior", *American Economic Review*, Vol. 53, No. 2, pp. 247-259.

JORGENSON, D.W., 1967. "The Theory of Investment Behavior", in R. Ferber (ed.), *Determinants of Investment Behavior*, New York: NBER and Columbia University Press.

JORGENSON, D.W., 1971. "Econometric Studies of Investment Behavior: A Survey", *Journal of Economic Literature*, Vol. 9, No. 4, pp. 1111-1147.

JORGENSON, D.W., 1974. "The Economic Theory of Replacement and Depreciation", in W. Sellekaerts (ed.), *Econometrics and Economic Theory, Essays in Honour of Jan Tinbergen*, London: Macmillan.

KENNEDY, K.A., 1971. *Productivity and Industrial Growth, The Irish Experience*, Oxford: Oxford University Press.

KING, M., 1974. "Taxation and the Cost of Capital", *Review of Economic Studies*, Vol. 41, No. 1, pp. 21-35.

MADDALA, G.S., 1977. *Econometrics*, New York: McGraw-Hill.

MEYER, J. and E. KUH, 1957. *The Investment Decision*, Cambridge, Mass.: Harvard University Press.

NEVIN, E., 1963. *The Capital Stock of Irish Industry,* Dublin: ESRI, Paper No. 17.

REDFERN, P., 1955. "Net Investment in Fixed Assets in the United Kingdom, 1938-1953", *Journal of the Royal Statistical Society*, Series A, Part 2, pp. 141-182.

ROBINSON, J., 1969. *The Accumulation of Capital* (Third edn.), London: Macmillan.

SHANLEY, L.F. and T. BOLAND, 1973. *Report on New House Prices*, National Prices Commission, Occasional Paper No. 2, Dublin: Stationery Office.

SLATTERY, D.G., 1974. "Fixed Capital Stock Estimation: An Empirical Exercise Using Irish Data", *Journal of the Statistical and Social Inquiry Society of Ireland*, Vol. XXIII, Part II.

Taxation on Industry, Committee of Inquiry Into, 1953, Report Prl. 3512, Dublin: Stationery Office.

TENGBLAD, A. and N. WESTERLUND, 1976. "Capital Stock and Capital Consumption Estimates by Industries in the Swedish National Accounts", *Review of Income and Wealth*, Series 22, No. 4, pp. 331-344.

UNITED NATIONS STATISTICAL OFFICE, 1974, 1976, 1977. *Yearbook of National Accounts Statistics*, Vol. 1, New York: United Nations Statistical Office.

WARD, M., 1976. *The Measurement of Capital, The Methodology of Capital Stock Estimates in OECD Countries*, Paris: OECD.

THE ECONOMIC AND SOCIAL RESEARCH INSTITUTE

Books:
Economic Growth in Ireland: The Experience Since 1947
Kieran A. Kennedy and Brendan Dowling

Irish Economic Policy: A Review of Major Issues
Staff Members of ESRI (eds. B. R. Dowling and J. Durkan)

Policy Research Series:
1. *Regional Policy and the Full-Employment Target*   M. Ross and B. Walsh
2. *Energy Demand in Ireland, Projections and Policy Issues*   S. Scott

Broadsheet Series:
1. *Dental Services in Ireland*   P. R. Kaim-Caudle
2. *We Can Stop Rising Prices*   M. P. Fogarty
3. *Pharmaceutical Services in Ireland*   P. R. Kaim-Caudle
    assisted by Annette O'Toole and Kathleen O'Donoghue
4. *Ophthalmic Services in Ireland*   P. R. Kaim-Caudle
    assisted by Kathleen O'Donoghue and Annette O'Toole
5. *Irish Pensions Schemes, 1969*   P. R. Kaim-Caudle and J. G. Byrne
    assisted by Annette O'Toole
6. *The Social Science Percentage Nuisance*   R. C. Geary
7. *Poverty in Ireland: Research Priorities*   Brendan M. Walsh
8. *Irish Entrepreneurs Speak for Themselves*   M. P. Fogarty
9. *Marital Desertion in Dublin: an exploratory study*   Kathleen O'Higgins
10. *Equalization of Opportunity in Ireland: Statistical Aspects*
    R. C. Geary and F. S. Ó Muircheartaigh
11. *Public Social Expenditure in Ireland*   Finola Kennedy
12. *Problems in Economic Planning and Policy Formation in Ireland, 1958—1974*
    Desmond Norton
13. *Crisis in the Cattle Industry*   R. O'Connor and P. Keogh
14. *A Study of Schemes for the Relief of Unemployment in Ireland*
    R. C. Geary and M. Dempsey
    with Appendix   E. Costa
15. *Dublin Simon Community, 1971—1976: an Exploration*   Ian Hart
16. *Aspects of the Swedish Economy and their relevance to Ireland*
    Robert O'Connor, Eoin O'Malley and Anthony Foley
17. *The Irish Housing System: A Critical Overview*   T. J. Baker and L. M. O'Brien
18. *The Irish Itinerants: Some Demographic, Economic and Educational Aspects*
    M. Dempsey and R. C. Geary
19. *A Study of Industrial Workers' Co-operatives*   Robert O'Connor and Philip Kelly

General Research Series
1. *The ownership of Personal Property in Ireland*   Edward Nevin
2. *Short-Term Economic Forecasting and its Application in Ireland*   Alfred Kuehn
3. *The Irish Tariff and The E.E.C.: A Factual Survey*   Edward Nevin

101

General Research Series—*continued*

General Research Series—*continued*